Peter Jensen & Mary Miles Minter & Mildred & Emma & Olga & Nancy
& Gertrude & Cindy & Tonya & Fanny & Sissy & Helena & Tina & Christina
& Mink & Candice-Marie & Jodie & Jytte & Laurie & Muriel & Shelley
& Anna Karina

This book is published on the occasion of the exhibition
Peter Jensen's Muses at the Designmuseum Danmark
5 August–30 October 2011

First published in the UK by Dent De Leone 2011
48 Wilton Way
E8 1BG London
www.dentdeleone.co.nz
ISBN 978-1-907908-04-0

All rights reserved. No part of this book may be reprinted, reproduced or
utilised in any form or by any electronic, mechanical or other means,
now known or hereafter invented, including photocopying and recording,
or in any information storage or retrieval system, without permission in
writing from the publishers.

Texts, images © the authors, all rights reserved in accordance with the
provisions of the copyright designs and patents act, 1988

Edited by Åbäke, Peter Jensen and Gerard Wilson
Designed by Åbäke
Set in Rr Medium
Proof read by Thomas Bush and The Wilsons
Printed by Die Keure, Belgium
Exhibition coordination by Line Rosenvinge

Thank you to Statens Kunst Fond for the work grant 2009–2011

This book has been kindly supported by Montana

A special thank you to:
Tina Barney
Frederik Bjerregaard
Jo-Ann Furniss
Eva Kruse
Joakim Lassen
Bodil Busk Laursen
Bryn Lloyd
Nikolina Olsen-Rule
Laurie Simmons
Mette Stagsted Larsen

Peter Jensen & Mary Miles Minter & Mildred & Emma & Olga & Nancy & Gertrude & Cindy & Tonya & Fanny & Sissy & Helena & Tina & Christina & Mink & Candice-Marie & Jodie & Jytte & Laurie & Muriel & Shelley & Anna Karina

Dent-De-Leone

CONTENTS

The Improbable Sisterhood of Peter Jensen
by Emily King 7

Peter Jensen's other women 21

Mary Miles Minter 25
Mildred 35
Emma 45
Olga 53
Nancy 63
Gertrude 69
Cindy 77
Tonya 89
Fanny 99
Sissy 111
Helena 125
Tina 137

Christina 147
Mink 157
Candice-Marie 167
Jodie 179
Jytte 189
Laurie 201
Muriel 215
Shelley 225
Anna Karina 233

The Life and Times of Peter Jensen
by Susannah Frankel 243

Index of music 264
Credits 268

The Improbable Sisterhood of Peter Jensen
by Emily King

After designing only menswear for the first two years of his career, Peter Jensen began making clothes for women in 2001. This move created the need for an imaginative focus. Where the primary decisions for men had been about the placement of buttons and the cut of a trouser leg, now he was confronted with thousands of possible stories. As Jensen's design partner Gerard Wilson explains, «It's much easier in womenswear to work out what you don't like than what you do.» So emerged the Peter Jensen muse, a coherent female image guiding each collection. «I regard my muses as a working tool,» says Jensen, «They also make it easier for me to explain my mindset. I love to talk about these women!» Over the last ten years twenty-one muses have been the cynosure for as many seasons.

«I like to believe that I select and research women who might never have been considered as fashion icons,» says Jensen. This is certainly true of his first muse, who as well as being his most obscure remains his favourite. Mary Miles Minter was born as Juliet Reilly in 1902. The daughter of an actress-turned-stage-mother, she was launched into full-time acting aged ten. Minter experienced the height of her success as a teenager, making over forty films between 1915 and 1920. Her soft, heart-shaped face epitomised the early twentieth century ideal and her expressive features won her silent screen success; but in spite of beauty and talent her star faded early. Aged just twenty Minter became involved in a scandal around the murder of the director William Desmond Taylor who, although 30 years her senior, was reputed to be her lover. Her career was cut short and she lived the rest of her days in Los Angeles, claiming never to have got over the love and loss of Taylor.

Jensen's curiosity about Minter was inspired by a fictionalised account of the Taylor murder. Less interested in the Minter of the ringlets and the Cupid's bow mouth, he was captivated by the thought of the aging former film star living among the trophies of her glory days and holding a candle for her long-dead amour. The photographs of the collection, Autumn/Winter 2001, were shot in the house of a friend's uncle in South London.
As in Jensen's imagined scenario of Minter's last years, the place was filled with objects that seem

to belong to another era. The framed portraits, decorative furniture and curtains resonate with the patterns, heavy fabric and offbeat formality of the clothes themselves. The look is that of a recluse who, anticipating a rare visit from the outside world, has dressed in her best.

To an extent Minter set the model for all the muses that followed. To be a Peter Jensen inspiration it is not enough to be a style icon, you must also have a backstory. Rather than looking at a woman as a whole, however, Jensen and Wilson tend to focus on a single chapter, or selected episodes in a character's life. These might be real or fictional, or a fuzzy confusion of the two. The designers are drawn to in-spite-of-itself glamour, looks that have all the ingredients to repulse, but are very attractive precisely because of that. It is the moment when Shelley Duvall (the muse of Spring/Summer 2011) playing Wendy Torrance in *The Shining*, eyes framed by her lank fringe, opens her mouth to scream. The image is look-and-look-again wrong.

The descriptions commonly applied to Jensen's muses and to the designer's style in general are humorous, nerdy and «with a twist». Jensen, meanwhile, who favours the apparently innocuous term «daywear», describes his clothes as «not obviously sexy» and views his women as unconventional and strong. This is all true, but alongside the low-key, off-kilter awkwardness and toughness common to his choices, there is also a streak of schadenfreude. Whether real or fictional, a Peter Jensen woman tends to be on her uppers. The result is an unmistakable tinge of callousness that cancels out the propensity toward the whimsical. In reviews of his collections it has been said over and over again that Peter Jensen's clothes make you smile. Perhaps so, but his humour is always offset by the looming presence of disaster.

Just as the Peter Jensen muses share certain essential qualities, so too do the garments. Gather together both icons and clothes and you have a pair of families united by a radical notion of resemblance. Jensen and Wilson have only recently begun to deliberately retread previous ground, to reuse shapes, fabrics and patterns, but even before the strategy became explicit, there was a distinctive quality to a Peter Jensen design. To put it crudely, everything is slightly wrong. Trousers are too short, armholes strain slightly and a very slight pull of fabric across the chest is offset by a crotch that hangs just low enough as to wrinkle each time you take a step. Other reoccurring traits are the thematic use of bold colour and the regular appearance of custom-designed patterns with strong motifs that create a subplot to the main story of the collection.

The overt celebration of the muse might imply that Peter Jensen clothes tend toward costume, but this isn't the case. They are more accurately seen as characters in themselves. Although the garments are very wearable, they stand slightly away from the body. They have an independent life; they tell their own tale. The ingredients of this quality are hard to pin down. While all Peter Jensen pieces have small oddities that might provoke curiosity or details that could raise a question, they are not bells-and-whistles avant garde. Instead of confronting the normal head on, they pull it slightly to one side, leaving it just a little skew-whiff.

Thinking of off-centre irregularity brings to mind the muse of Spring/Summer 2003, the Soviet gymnast Olga Korbut who, at height of her success in the early 1970s, was adored as much for her unkempt appearance as she was for her athleticism. Running against the Western understanding of Soviet regimentation and apparently unselfconscious, Korbut's look was probably as controlled as her floor work. Unlike Minter, she didn't meet a particular calamity, but the fleeting form of young gymnasts and the undertones of exploitation that cling to their training generate a halo of tragedy around them even while they're at their peak.

Pursuing the athletic theme, Jensen also made a muse of Tonya Harding, the figure skater who was implicated in the hobbling of her rival Nancy Kerrigan and then had a second career in women's boxing. Where the Olga collection hinged on appealingly runkled sportswear in greys and brights, Tonya (Spring/Summer 2005) was a spin on sweats and frills rendered in deliciously lurid colours and modelled by ice skaters.

Much more sober and literary were Nancy (Nancy Mitford, Autumn/Winter 2003) and Gertrude (Gertrude Stein, Spring/Summer 2004), both of them being more about a period—early interwar in the case of Gertrude, late interwar in the case of Nancy—than specific biographies. Likewise

Helena (Helena Rubinstein, Autumn/Winter 2006) and Muriel (Muriel Sparke, Autumn/Winter 2010) seem to be about the formality and restraint of bygone eras, in Helena's case backcombed and tweedy and in Muriel's tartan and uniformed.

More oddball «real-life» muses include Christina (Christina of Denmark, Autumn/Winter 2007), a sixteenth century princess, the only surviving image of whom is a painting by Hans Holbein. Showing the 16-year old in sober velvets and fur, the portrait was intended to advertise her to Henry VIII. Myth has it that she rejected the English King's advances on the grounds she didn't have a head to spare. Attracted by the painting and the story, Jensen and Wilson used Christina as a pretext to explore modest clothes in extravagant fabrics. In particular, they experimented with cutting on the bias, a more wasteful way to tailor clothes that was once a means of signalling wealth.

Even further out on a limb as a muse is Jensen's own aunt Jytte (pronounced You-da, Autumn/Winter 2009). A hard-living, pleasure loving woman who ran a series of small businesses in Greenland, Jytte caught her nephew's imagination with her propensity to wear mini skirts in the depths of the northern winter. The collection began life during a research trip to Greenland and caused controversy by making explicit reference to traditional dress. Much to Jensen and Wilson's surprise, a group of around thirty women took to the streets of Greenland's capital Nuuk to protest against their abuse of folkloric embroidery. Until 1979 Greenland was a colony of Denmark and, hard though it is to imagine, the gentle, softly spoken Jensen was viewed as a cultural marauder.

Needlework is an unlikely subject for a ruckus, but given his taste for compromised glamour Jensen always runs the risk of making references that might touch nerves. Discussing future muses in the late winter of 2011, against the background of uprisings in the Middle East, Wilson admitted an attraction to the risky territory of deposed dictators' wives. The most tasteless of all Peter Jensen muses is indubitably Mink Stole, but her collection (Spring/Summer 2008) is uncontroversial, the inspiration being a composite of characters rather than the sixty-something actress herself. On the runway Stole's best known costumes, such as the babydoll nightie worn by overgrown child Taffy Davenport in John Waters's *Female Trouble*, lose their grubbiness but keep the bite of impropriety.

Other actress/composite character muses include the aforementioned Shelley, Sissy (Sissy Spacek, Spring/Summer 2006), Jodie (Jodie Foster, Spring/Summer 2009) and most recently Anna Karina (Autumn/Winter 2011). Relishing the loss of definition that comes when an actress is merged with her roles, the press release for the Jodie collection imagines a conversation between the Foster character Clarice Starling and the serial killer Hannibal Lecter of the 1991 horror classic *The Silence of the Lambs*. The form of the exchange implies psychological game playing, but the content is leopard prints and balloon sleeves.

In actively blurring the boundary between the fictional and real, Jensen and Wilson appear on occasion to have fallen victim to their own confusion. From time to time they have sent clothes to the actresses in question and admit to feeling disappointed when their gifts go unacknowledged. On a similar note, Wilson claims to be attracted to the idea of a flesh-and-blood muse, «an independently wealthy woman who lives at the Ritz», but concedes that his and Jensen's face-to-face encounters with their inspirations have in the past been disconcerting. Visiting the photographer Tina Barney, for example, whose work inspired the Spring/Summer 2007

collection, the pair arrived at her New York apartment with cake and champagne.
She refused both slice and glass, but insisted they eat and drink, making them both feel incredibly uncomfortable. Just desserts, perhaps, for designers who fetishise the awkward.

The nature of the relationship between the muse and the collection varies a great deal from season to season. There are some very direct references—for example the frilled shirt worn by the young Sissy Spacek in *Badlands*—but often the connection is elusive. Tracing Jensen's line of thought in the development of the Mildred collection (Spring/Summer 2002) might be hardest of all. Based on Bette Davis's volatile character in the film *Of Human Bondage*, beyond a suggestion of bed jackets and nightgowns, clothes worn by Davis in the film's climatic scenes, it's hard to find the thread. The collection is perhaps most notable for the birth of the Peter Jensen rabbit motif, which has since become a de facto trademark.

As well as the rabbit, Jensen has included images of giraffes, foxes, dogs and polar bears in his designs, all stylised to various degrees. The pairing of animal and muse is often confusing (why giraffes for Nancy Mitford?), but Jensen insists, «Despite their seemingly random appeal, they are carefully considered. It is important to choose the right animal for the collection.» Perhaps the most important function of the Peter Jensen menagerie is to create an element of lightness that offsets his muses' tendency toward the dark. «I will never be that designer who creates something morbid and depressing,» says Jensen, «Fashion for me is a luxury and about feeling good, so I see no point in making it sad and negative.» And, as Jensen says, «Isn't it just super cosy to wear a picture of an animal?»

I have spent hours at my computer tracing Jensen and Wilson's inspirations, searching names and images and watching YouTube. As I tip-tapped away, I had imagined the designers doing pretty much the same thing first time round, but later discovered that they had gone digital relatively recently. «Ten years ago, when we began, we didn't even have a computer. I think we had a typewriter,» says Wilson. Instead of typing in image searches and watching film clips, they were drawn to the subjects of biographies, newspaper articles and TV documentaries—sources Wilson calls «English and dreary». Describing the triumph of Google as «good and bad,» he says «Everything seems more available, which makes it feel less special, but I can´t really imagine a world before image search or Wikipedia now.»

Apart from search engines, Wilson argues that technology has played its most significant role to date in facilitating their collaboration with the New York-based artist Laurie Simmons (Spring/Sumer 2010). Corresponding via e-mail, the designers made scaled down versions of their garments; arranged to have them photographed in one of Simmons's dollhouse environments (the artist has worked in miniature since the early 1980s); and then used these images as the bases for a new set of human scale clothes. Simmons, Jensen and Wilson met for the first time at the presentation of the collection at the Institute of Contemporary Arts in London. The biggest clue to the derivation of the garments is the larger than usual patterns and boxy construction. As with every Peter Jensen collection, Laurie represents a step into fantasy, but in this instance the alternative world was constructed rather than merely imagined.

Although Laurie Simmons's relationship with the Laurie collection is exceptional, she, like the other

Peter Jensen muses, was the force that propelled the season's story. For Jensen and Wilson the appointment of a new muse every six months is crucial in generating the momentum for the next collection and enabling them to meet fashion's demand for novelty. While many designers regard the constant need for renewal as a curse, Jensen and Wilson welcome the chance to sweep away the old references and start with a fresh model. The six-monthly clean out, the process of taking down images from the studio wall, organising them into a scrap book and filing them away, is something they look forward to. Perhaps even too much: reviewing the past twenty-one seasons, while there is some consistency, the changes from one collection to the next can be extreme. From Christina's heavy fabrics and dark colours to Mink's bright vulgarity, or Jodie's tomboy charm to Jytte's folklorism, often fashion writers and buyers find it hard to keep up.

When I spoke to Jensen and Wilson in preparation for writing this piece they had just presented Anna Karina and were about to start work on the new collection (Spring/Summer 2012.) While there was a scent of a certain style of muse in the air, nothing had been decided. The designers say it can be difficult pin down their inspiration, but that is more about their need for precision than a lack of suitable candidates. Conversations with the pair of them veer pleasantly from one wildly interesting woman to another. Twenty-one muses down, it appears that there are still many more strong, dangerous and challenging women to explore. So many potential muses, so little time.

More muses, clockwise from top left: Charlotte Mann, Kajsa Ståhl, Julie Verhoeven (Eva Sajovic) and Beth Fenton

Clockwise from top left: Nina Persson (Graham Willoughby), Shirley Kurata (Autumn de Wilde), Emily King, Natascha Stolle, Connie Chan, Chris Feshias, Christine Muller, Ann-Sofie Back (Marcus Palmquist)

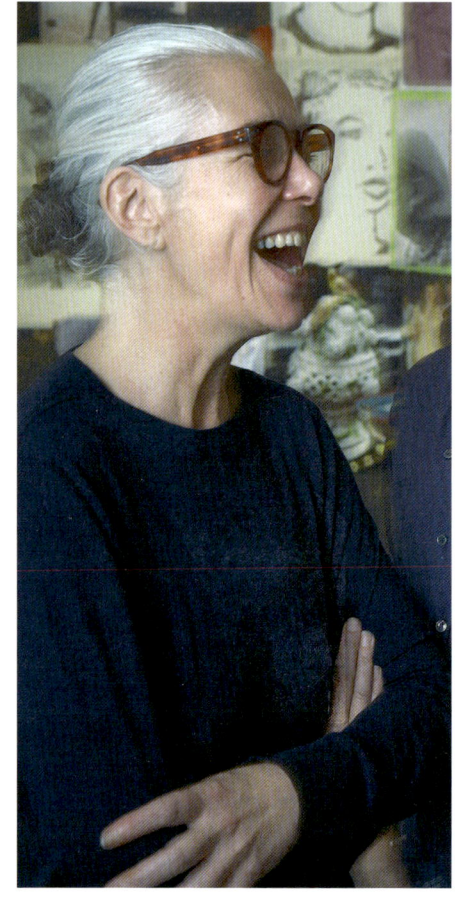

Clockwise from top left: Yuko Suwahara, Thelma Speirs (Daniel Schweitzer), Kathryn Dale, Vanessa Tao, Susannah Frankel

Annie Kevans

MARY MILES MINTER
(Born Juliet Reilly; April 1, 1902, Shreveport, Louisiana—August 4, 1984.)

The daughter of a Broadway actress, Minter was given her first acting role at the age of five, and her first feature film role at thirteen.

It was *Anne of Green Gables*, the first film she made with director William Desmond Taylor, that made her a star. A romantic relationship developed between her and Taylor, though he ended the affair, citing the thirty-year age difference as the reason.

In 1922, Taylor was murdered; the long investigation that ensued counted Minter and her mother amongst the suspects, and though neither of them was ever charged, the speculation and media coverage left Minter with a scandalous reputation. Her studio contract was never renewed and she gave up acting, living only on real estate investments she made in Los Angeles. She died in Santa Monica in 1984 from a stroke.

Minter has a Star on the Hollywood Walk of Fame at 1724 Vine Street.

Rhys Moore

MILDRED
(Portrayed by Bette Davis in John Cromwell's *Of Human Bondage*, 1934)

Mildred is an illiterate tearoom waitress who catches the eye of failed artist Philip Carey. Carey (who is club-footed) is insulted by Mildred on every attempt to make his sentiments known. Despite this, he becomes more and more distracted by her, to the point where he fails his medical exams.

Mildred refuses to marry Carey, and marries loutish salesman Emil Miller instead. The marriage doesn't last and she returns to Carey, pregnant and abandoned.

Eventually Mildred agrees to wed, but quickly becomes bored. On the night of their engagement party she flirts with one of Carey's friends and subsequently runs off with him. She returns sometime later, once more abandoned, and is taken in yet again by Carey. But in a fit of anger she destroys his belongings and disappears.

Time passes and Mildred reappears, now a prostitute with tuberculosis. Her child is dead. In the final reel, Mildred dies in the charity ward of a local hospital, alone.

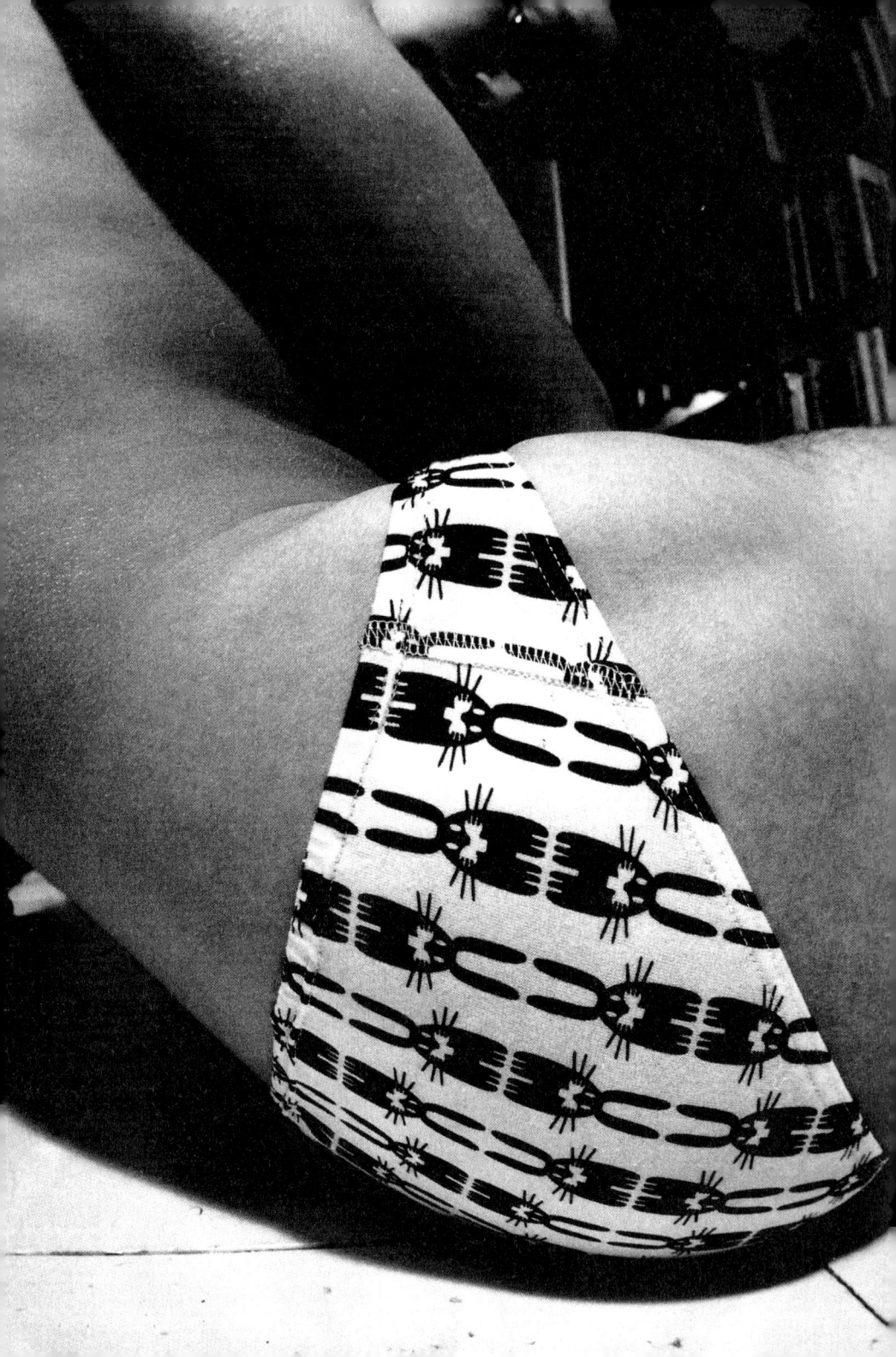

Peter Jensen
«Mildred»

Peter Jensen «Emma»

Autumn / Winter 2002
Invitation

Wednesday 20th February
4.30 pm
The Brompton Oratory
Brompton Road
(at the junction of Thurloe Place)
SW7

Pressagent: Jay Thompson
2nd floor, 4-8 Rodney Street
London N1 9JH
Tel: 020 74 27 24 55
Fax: 020 74 27 24 56

sponsored by TODD & DUNCAN

Suzie Foster

EMMA

Emma Cook grew up between Glossop and Manchester. Her mother is a hairdresser and cuts her daughter's bleached-blonde tresses to this day. Her father worked for Rowntree Mackintosh and then Boddingtons before becoming a musician.

Their daughter's fashion education began at Brighton University. Following graduation, she was accepted on to the fashion MA course at Central Saint Martins and, with the course's formidable and legendary director, Louise Wilson, she travelled to New York to complete a stint with Donna Karan. She graduated in 1999, set up her own line and immediately attracted considerable attention.

«She's always been the same,» says Cathy Edwards, fashion director of *Another Magazine*, who styles Cook's twice-yearly shows. «She works really, really hard. She was the youngest person in our year because she skipped her foundation course and she always got the best marks. She thinks of an idea and then she gets really excited about it. I come in and she's like, «Look, look, it's latex! But it's tie-dyed! It's amazing!»

Edwards sums up the look of her friend's clothes thus: «So a girl will be out in a dress and it will seem quite simple. And another girl will say, «That's nice, but what's that?» pointing to a wooden carving on her shoulder. And then the girl will say, «It's a wooden owl, actually, it's hand-carved». And her friend will say, «Lovely.»

fashion & style

Great Dane

It's funny how it takes a Scandinavian with a hint of a Yorkshire accent and an obsession with Mike Leigh and all things British to come up with some of London's most radical creations. But then Peter Jensen is no ordinary designer, as **JO-ANN FURNISS** discovers

When first approaching Peter Jensen's clothing you might be fooled into thinking that his beautifully produced menswear and womenswear is at the more conventional, traditional end of British design. But, as Jensen himself puts it, "I'm quite obsessive about the small things. You really have to look at the stuff to fully appreciate it." Then he'll start telling you how shirts with ruched collars from a past season were "inspired by Lee Miller's pictures of hung men in World War Two prisons". Or how one collection was "based on a silent film actress's suicide". Or how he has an ongoing interest in "the child murderess Mary Bell". At this point, you might nervously start to back away from him.

In fact, what Jensen endlessly dissects and most often combines are the extreme sides of British culture in his clothing. For summer there was "Mildred" (his collections are always named after women), whose chief inspiration was the downbeat, Depression-era madness of Bette Davis's cockney character in *Of Human Bondage*. It was her smudged make-up, slip-dressed look, aligned with a slightly sinister print of interlinking rabbits (as he says, you really have to look to see) which skewed what, on the surface, was a conservative collection. With his latest offering for autumn/winter 2002, "Emma", there seems as much of the film-director Mike Leigh in its aesthetic as there is of that quintessentially English aristo, Nancy Mitford - from his "Meantime" menswear separates with their geeky charm, to the "Cold Climate" stolid elegance of the womenswear.

Not bad for a young designer who hails from Scandinavia. Peter Jensen comes from a small fishing town called Logstor on the coast of Denmark. Not surprisingly, he says: "I always felt like an outsider there. I think that was one of the reasons I have always been attracted to Britain." But this is not the usual kind of ham-fisted cultural tourism that fashion is at times so adept at, the "I-went-on-holiday-to-India-got-amoebic-dysentery-and-made-my-collection-pink" school of thought. Peter Jensen often has a keener sense of what Britain is about than many British people. He is also part of a loose grouping of designers who are redefining the spirit of London fashion.

Gone are the days of the pointy, spiky, you'll-have-an-eye-out-with-that-lapel aggression found in the "London Look" of the Nineties. In its stead comes a more subtle but no less eccentric mood, low on accident-prone tailoring, yet high on radical inspiration. It's a new feeling that can be found in Jensen's clothes as well as in the work of designers as disperate as Emma Cook, Blaak, Russell Sage and Eley Kishimoto, to name but a few. And, as might be garnered from their names, this is a new international mood where crafty cockneys and mockneys are a bit thin on the ground, just as they are in music these days.

Having lived in London since 1997, completing his MA in menswear at Central Saint Martins College in 1999, Peter Jensen now feels truly at home in Britain. He appreciated the everyday oddness of the place and it is this mood that often infiltrates the clothes. This is despite the fact that it is not the Mike Leigh/Alan Clarke paradise he had previously dreamed of, peopled by Ritas, Sues and Bobs too. "I have to say, after seeing that film I thought 'I'm moving there'," says the 30-year-old designer of his misspent youth mulling over the British class system at the movies. Some of his subsequent collection have even been named after Mike Leigh's leading ladies, including "Alison" as in Steadman and "Brenda" for Blethyn. "It's a shame that people just look at class ironically instead of with genuine interest and see the brilliance in it. In Scandinavia the class system has all but gone and it is very blanded out, in a way. Everybody is equal but I don't think there is the ambition and drive to do something different that happens here. I admire people because of that ambition, of wanting change and something better. There is no ambition whatsoever in Scandinavia." Yet ambition is something this particular designer has in spades.

Jensen began making clothes at the ripe old age of 12 – at his local sewing circle, no less. "It was all female OAPs except for me," he explains. "I went with my sister. We had to go every Thursday with a sewing machine and sew for two hours. The women would come with cakes and coffee and make their own clothes. I used to make garments for my neighbour. She was very fat and couldn't find any clothes in the shops to fit her. As time went on, the fatter she became, the bigger and bigger the garments grew. The neck grew up and up as well, because she wanted to hide. This was quite a challenge." It may also explain why his clothes are now very forgiving. In the following years, his mania to learn different techniques grew and what followed were stints at embroidery school – "there were 80 women, all female tutors and me" – two years being taught tailoring, life-drawing classes, a BA in fashion design, and then eventually his MA in London.

It is perhaps no surprise that what marks out Jensen's clothing is a rigorous attention to technique and fine detailing. When asked which fashion house he would ideally like to design for, he replies without hesitation: "Jean Muir. Her own designs were fantastic." This fits perfectly with his ethos. His approach has also made him one

> **'JENSEN ALWAYS ADDS LITTLE JOKES TO CLOTHES THAT ARE ESSENTIALLY VERY CLASSIC IN THEIR WAY'**

fashion

Peter Jensen with Jayne Roberts, the senior buyer at the London store 'b' (main picture); clothes from his autumn/winter collection (above and inset left)

of the most successful young London designers in terms of sales. As Jayne Roberts, senior buyer at "b" puts it: "Peter is a buyer's dream. He fits a commercial brief with his strict attention to craftsmanship. At the same time, there is always a certain quirkiness and little jokes added to clothes that are essentially very classic in their way. From his first collection what he was doing was very complete and together, which is very unusual for such a new designer. He's the best seller in our shop."

After the crash, bang, wallop that accompanied many of the next big thing London designers of the Nineties, it is this more low-key – and, dare I say it? – commercial approach that seems to be winning in the economic climate of the moment. It has tempered many of those emerging from Saint Martins in recent years who have also found that careers can be as easily wrecked by media hype as made. It is a view that could be seen to be shared by many of Jensen's peer group from the college, including his friend and fellow designer Emma Cook (who was on the womenswear MA at the same time).

Unusually, his latest collection is named after her. The designer explains: "When I first met Emma, I thought she was really rude. She was eating a bag of crisps at the time and tossed the empty packet on the table in front of me. I thought, 'How terrible!' and never spoke to her again for a year." Jensen is full of these slightly Alan Bennett-like monologues (he has a mild Yorkshire accent to boot). He continues: "Anyway, I like her now, even though she makes really trashy things for English sluts. She says my clothes are for 'weeping vaginas' – for mums and nuns. The last collection came out of insults like that. She's an inspiration." There follows a characteristic, slightly warped giggle.

Needless to say, this is not the usual non-committal line taken by designers when they are discussing their peers. Conveniently, in the next studio sits Emma Cook herself. "Peter has probably said I make clothes for slags, hasn't he?" she queries, laughing. Such easy familiarity is not often on display in the world of young, ambitious designers, but perhaps this is also part of the new spirit to be found in London fashion now. Long may it continue.

Peter Jensen is stocked at "b", 6 Conduit Street, London W1 (020-7499 6628)

Kirsty wears suit and shirt by
shoes by Yo

Like someone watching over me

PHOTOGRAPHY BY ROBERT WYATT
STYLING BY LUCY EWING

Hair by Fernando Torrent using KMS
Make-up by Liz Daxauer at CAN
Photographic assistance by Neil Bridge and Richie Hopson
Styling assistance by Susie Rushton
Models: Kirsty Hume at Premier, Tom, Aubrey and Briony

Suzie Foster

OLGA
Olga Korbut (Born May 16, 1955, Hrodna; known as the Sparrow from Minsk)

Olga began training in gymnastics at the age of eight and joined the Belarusian sports school at the age of eleven. Her first competition was at the USSR championships in 1969, where she ended in fifth position. Due to illness and injury she did not compete much until the 1972 Summer Olympics.

Her performance at this event enraptured the audiences—her routines being highly acrobatic and often with displays of emotion—very unusual for athletes from the Eastern Bloc. It was at these games that she became one of the first people to do a backward somersault on the balance beam in competition, as well as being the first to do a standing backward somersault on bars and a back somersault to swing down on beam, later called the Korbut Flip. The back tuck and the Korbut Flip are still very popular in gymnastics.

Her return to the Olympics in 1976 was not as successful, though she gained a team gold medal, and a silver medal for balance beam. After moving to America to escape the Soviet Union, no longer a competitive gymnast, Korbut slipped into obscurity.

Peter Jensen
«Nancy»

Invitation for the Autumn Winter collection 2003, Wednesday 19th of February 2003 at 1pm at Cinema Lumière, 17 Queensbury Place, London SW7, off Cromwell road. The nearest tube is South Kensington. You will be sitting Block   , Row

William Acton

NANCY
Nancy Freeman Mitford CBE (28 November, 1904, London – 30 June, 1973).

Nancy was the eldest daughter of Lord Redesale, whose daughters became famous as the Mitford sisters. Nancy was known for her writing, the first amongst the sisters to make public the very English and very eccentric life of her family.

After a bizarre romance with the homosexual Scottish aristocrat Hamish St. Clair-Erskine, and a disastrous marriage to the Hon. Peter Rodd, it was Mitford's affair with Colonel Gaston Palewski that inspired her most famous novel, *The Pursuit of Love*.

The romance between them carried on until he married Violette de Talleyrand-Perigord, the Duchess of Sagan, in 1969. In 1972 she was awarded the titles of Commander of the Order of the British Empire and Officer in the French Legion of Honour. She died of Hodgkin's disease on 30 June, 1973 in Versailles. Palewski was with her on the day she died.

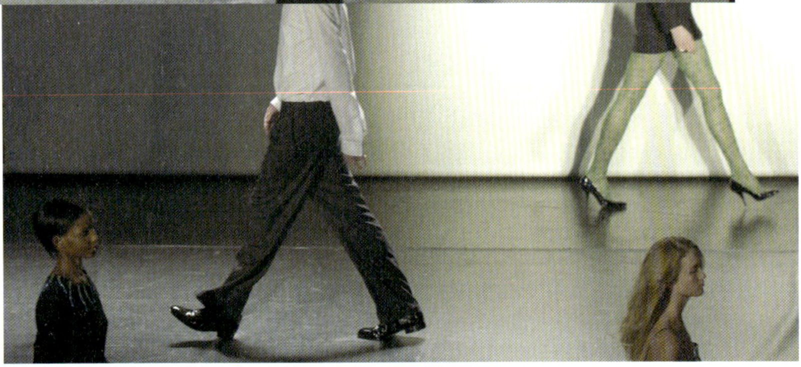

Peter Jensen «Gertrude»   Invitation for the Spring / Summer 2004 collection

Wednesday 24 September, 9.30 am, 9 Grosvenor Place, London SW1X 7SH.
Block____ Row____ Seat____

69

Linus Sundahl-Djerf

GERTRUDE

Gertrude Stein (born February 3, 1874- Allegheny, Pennsylvania – July 27, 1946).

After her parents' death, Stein's eldest brother sent her and her sister Bertha to live with relatives in Baltimore. During this time, she met Claribel and Etta Cone, who held Saturday evening salons, which Gertrude later emulated in Paris.

She studied psychology, but became famous for the private art collection she amassed with her brother Leo Stein, as well as for her fiercely modernist writing, and for her relationship with Alice B. Toklas. They met in Paris in 1907 and were together for the rest of Stein's life.

Stein is also known for being one of the earliest authors to pen a «coming out» story, based on her travels after leaving college, and a three person affair she joined while at Johns Hopkins in Baltimore. She suppressed the publication for 47 years, but was it eventually published posthumously in 1950 under the name «Things as They Are».

At the age of 72, Stein passed away in Neuilly-sur-Seine, after suffering stomach cancer, and was interred at Père Lachaise cemetery.

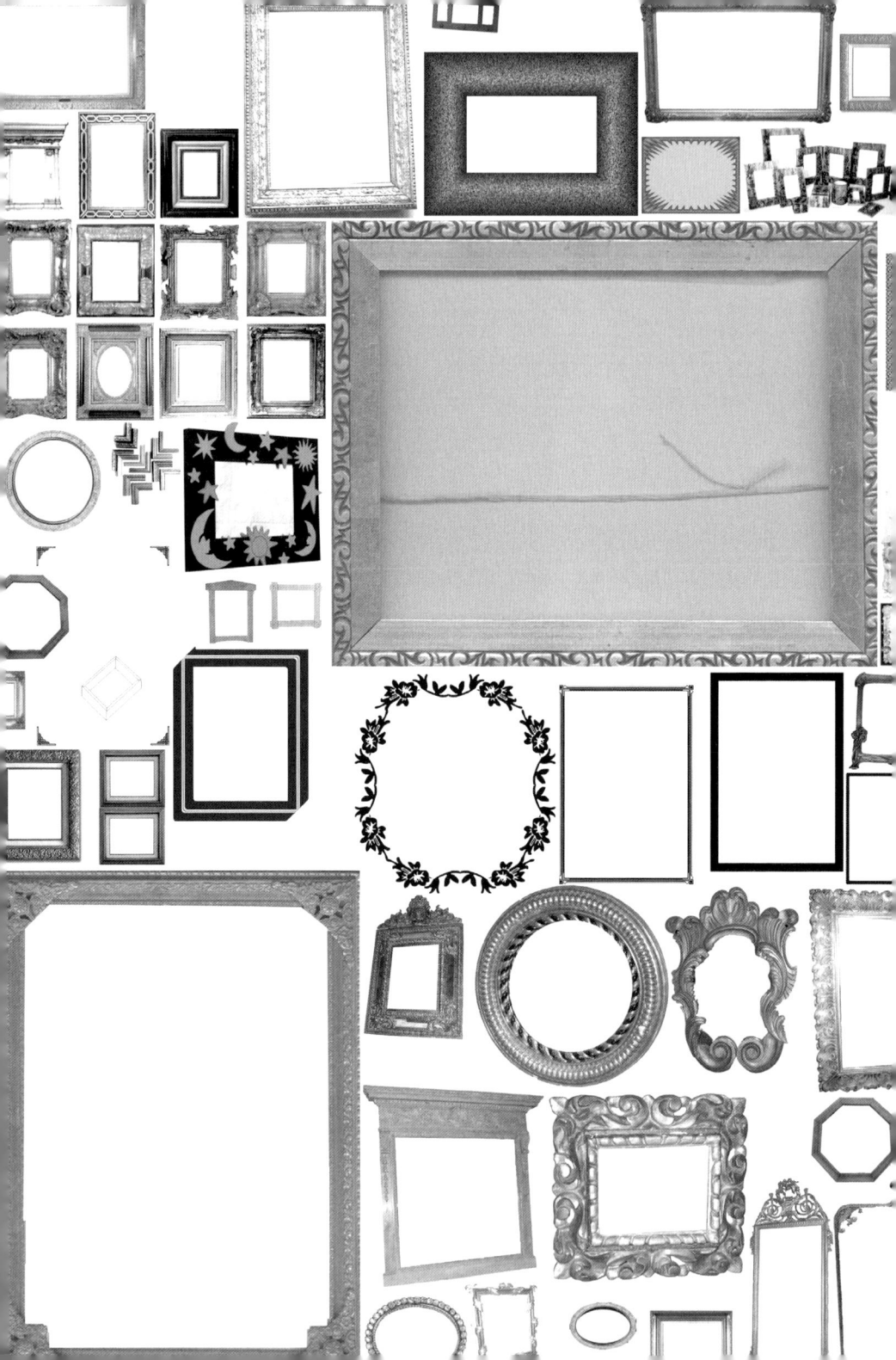

Peter Jensen
« Cindy »

<u>Invitation</u> for the
Autumn / Winter 2004–05 collection
Monday 16 February, 3.45pm
Baden Powell House,
65–67 Queen's gate, London SW7 5JS

<u>Press Enquiries:</u>
Andrew Leahy at Cube,
T: 020 7242 5483, F: 020 7242 5454,
E: andrew@cubecompany.com

<u>Sales Enquiries:</u>
Gerard Wilson at Peter Jensen,
T: 020 7249 6894, F: 020 7249 5858,
E: mail@peterjensenltd.com

<u>Sales Japan:</u>
Zeniya inc, T: +81 3 3780 6851

Viola Renate

CINDY

Cindy Sherman (born 1954, Glen Ridge, New Jersey) was educated at Buffalo State College, enrolling in the basic studio courses—drawing, painting and photography. Sherman initially failed the required photography class, having trouble with the technical side. Later, she was inspired to «just take pictures».

After graduation, she decided to move to New York City to embark upon a career in art. Taking a loft on Fulton Street in lower Manhattan, Sherman began taking photographs of herself, most famously in the series *Untitled Film Stills*.

Sherman does not consider her work feminist, and she is not a fan of museums: «Even when I was doing those history pictures, I was living in Rome but never went to the churches and museums there. I worked out of books, with reproductions. It's an aspect of photography I appreciate, conceptually: the idea that images can be reproduced and seen any time, anywhere, by anyone.»

PHOTOGRAPHY **ROBERT MONTGOMERY**
STYLING **JULIE TELFER**

Costume

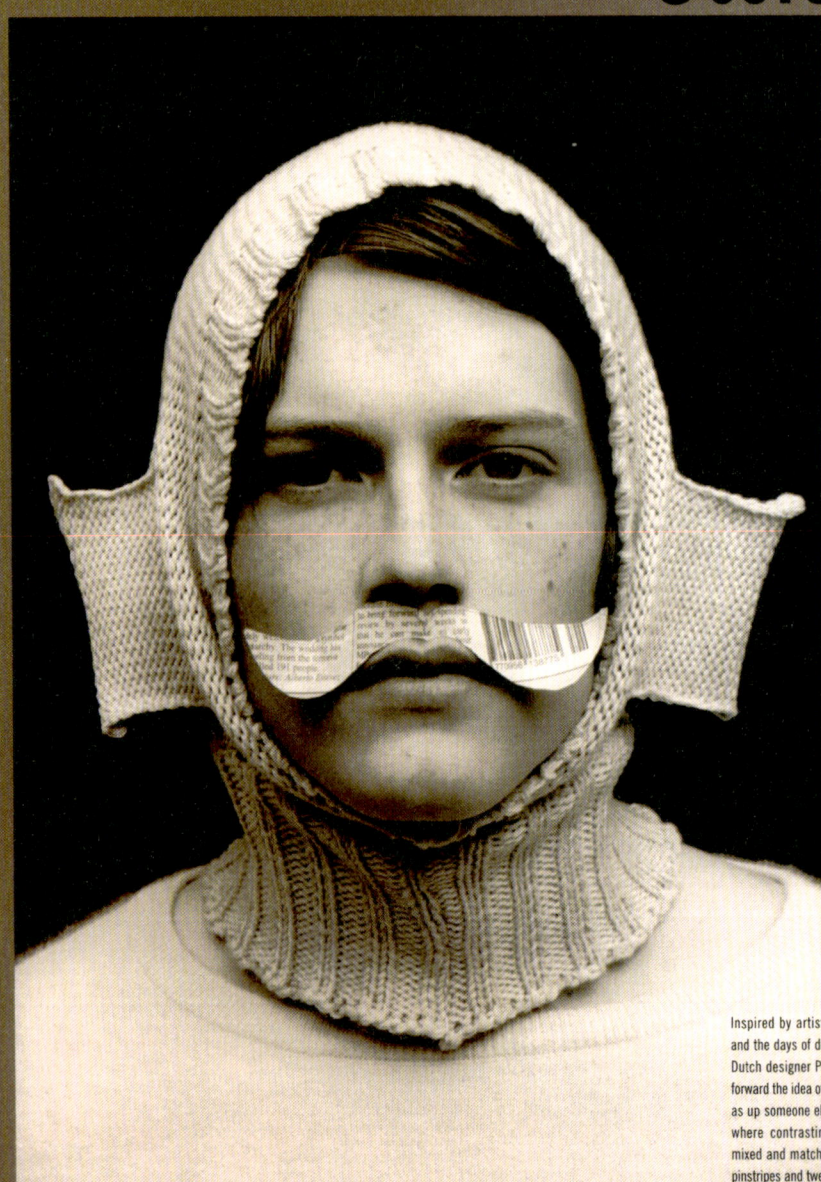

Inspired by artist Cindy Sherman and the days of dressing-up, Dutch designer Peter Jensen puts forward the idea of dressing as up someone else in a collection where contrasting materials are mixed and matched. Sweat shirts, pinstripes and tweeds meet crystals and sequins for the designer's eclectic A/W collection. AM

MODEL ALISTAIR WILSON AT MODELS 1 SPECIAL THANKS TO ANDREW LEAHY AND GERARD WILSON

ALL CLOTHES BY PETER JENSEN.

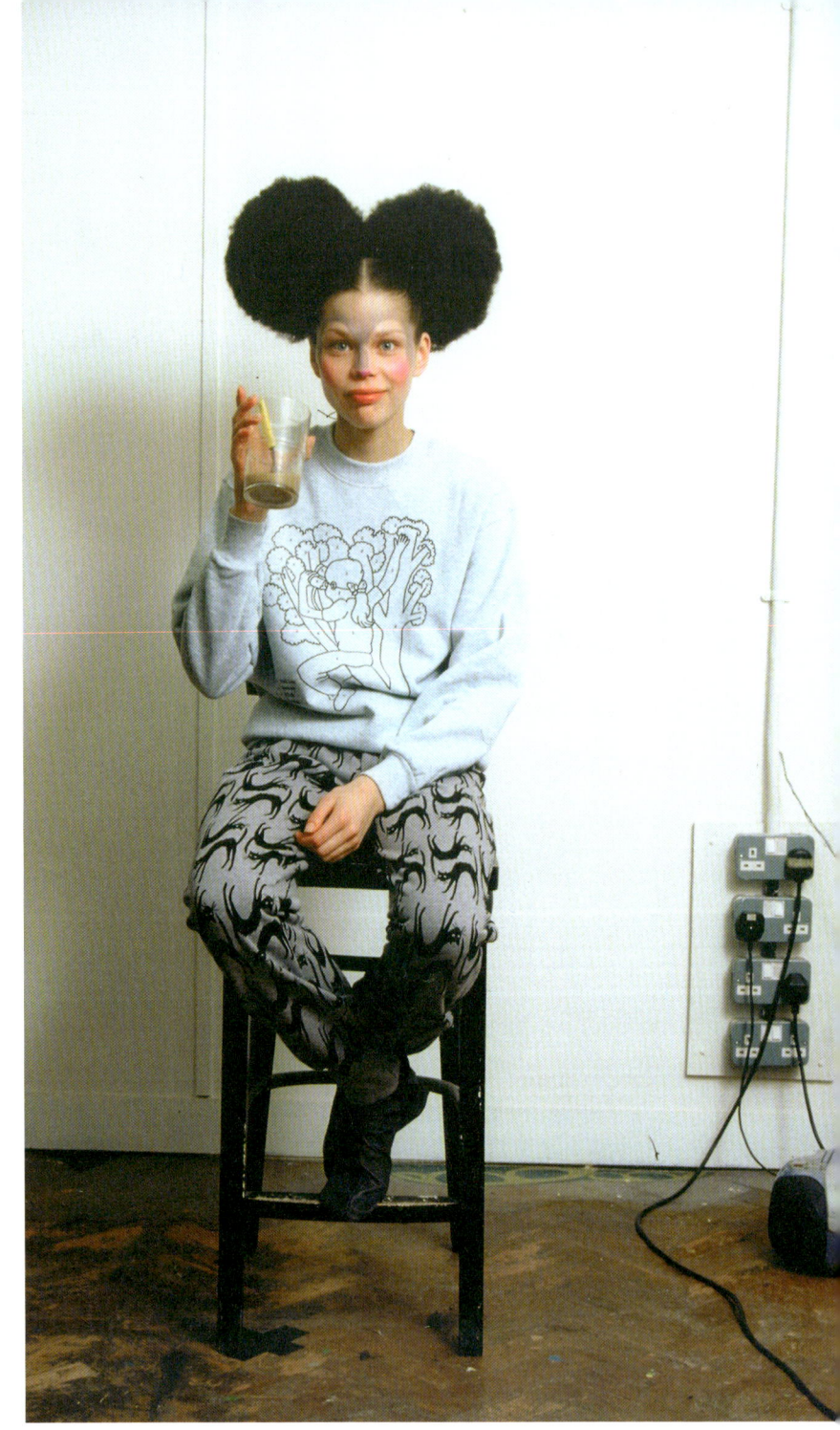

Dame Darcy

TONYA
Tonya Harding (born November 12th 1970, Portland, Oregon).

Following her parents' divorce, Harding dropped out of high school and started to pursue figure skating as a career. She was the first U.S. woman to land the triple axel in competition, completing it 45 seconds into her free skate at the 1991 U.S. championships.

Harding's career was marked with a series of accidents and incidents. Some television commentators remarked that no competition was complete without her having a crisis. In 1994 this reputation was cemented when she became a suspect in the vicious attack on her competitor Nancy Kerrigan. Ten years after skating at the Lillehammer Olympic Games, Tonya Harding hung up her boots and took up boxing.

Tonya would like to make enough money boxing then retire to live alone with her Persian cat, Smalls. «[A perfect life] would be having enough money to go hunting and fishing and go to the big four-wheel-drive mud bogs,» she says. «And every once in a while put on a really pretty dress and go to dinner at a place like Applebee's or something.»

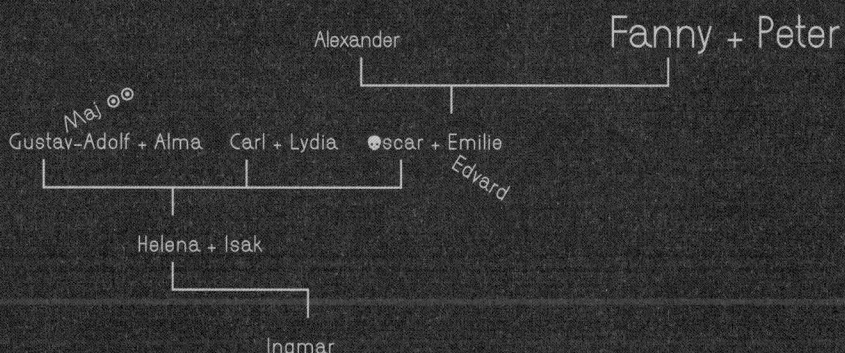

FANNY
Fanny Ekdahl (portrayed by Pernilla Allwin in Ingmar Bergman's *Fanny och Alexander*, 1982).

Fanny and her brother Alexander are the youngest members of the well-to-do Ekdahl family, growing up in a Swedish town during the early 1900s. The Ekdahl parents are both involved in theatre, and are happily married, until the father's sudden death from a stroke. Shortly thereafter, their mother, Emilie, finds a new suitor in the local bishop, and accepts his proposal of marriage, moving into his ascetic home and putting the children under his stern and unforgiving rule.

The children and their mother live as virtual prisoners in the bishop's house until finally the Ekdahl family intervenes, urged by Emilie who has secretly been in touch with her former mother-in-law and has told her of their dire situation. Fanny is the quieter character; her brother Alexander is the focus of the movie.

peter jensen **designer**

In your own words, what do you do? Design clothes **What inspires you to work?** I've always liked working; I don't like to be idle **What was your big break?** I think the ice skating show last spring-summer made a big difference **Who and what is most essential to what you do?** The people I work with **Can you name five different jobs that you have held in your life?** Gardener, lifeguard, McDonalds, carer in an old people's home and designer **What might people be surprised to learn about your occupation?** How little money you make **What are the dangers of your job?** Being overworked **Best and worst career point?** This is my best career point. I think my worst was changing old men's catheters.

alex box **make-up artist**

What do you do? Artist, psychiatrist, anthropologist **What inspires you to work?** To create something as simple and as perfect as nature **What was your big break?** An i-D beauty story and interview **Who and what is most essential to your work?** The love of a good man, the love of a good agent **Can you name five different jobs you have held?** Picture framer, purveyor of gothic goods, royal waitress, display artist, paper girl **What might people be surprised to learn about your occupation?** How heavy my bags are **What are the dangers of your occupation?** See above **Best and worst career point?** Being moved to tears by what I do/being moved to tears by what I do.

SHOT BACKSTAGE AT PETER JENSEN'S A/W '05 SHOW
PHOTOGRAPHY BY PAUL BLISS

HONEY v BUNNY

MADRID GETS THIS

LONDON GETS THIS

By **TONI JONES**, Sun Fashio...

IT'S every model's worst nightmare — a bad hare day at London Fashion Week.

One girl stunned catwalk watchers by wearing a bright blue bunny mask and floppy ears, *below*.

She must have wished she was working at a show in Madri... sexy senoritas paraded thei... in see-through outfits, *left*.

Peter Jensen was the desig... gave new meaning to t... bunny girl at his show.

But she ended up looki... like a reject from a Disney

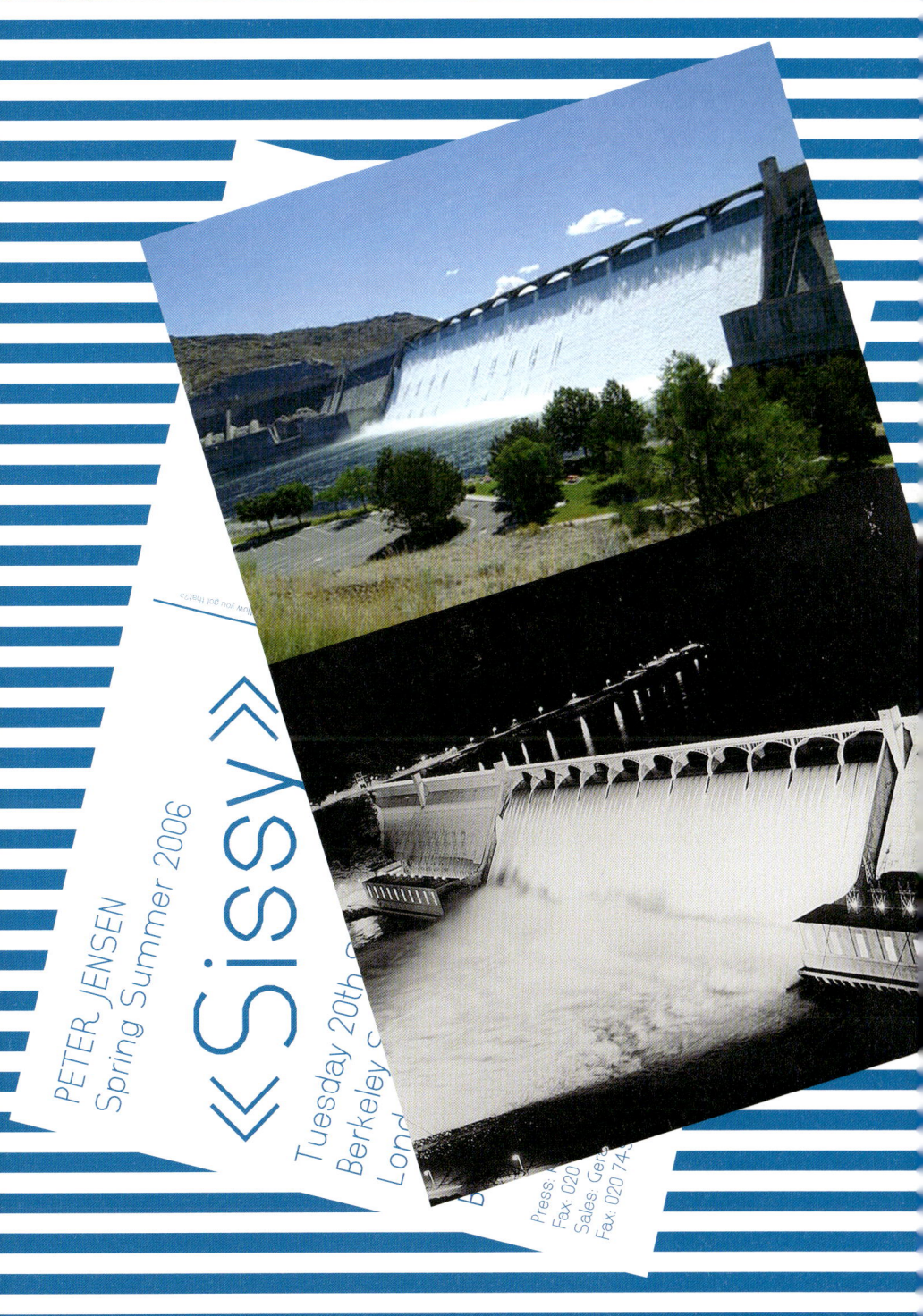

Mark Collishaw

SISSY
Mary Elizabeth «Sissy» Spacek (born December 25, 1949, Quitman, Texas).

Sissy Spacek's cousin, Rip Torn, sparked her interest in acting, and through him she enrolled in the New York branch of the Actors' Studio. Whilst studying under Lee Strasberg she worked as an itinerant model and singer, appearing in West Village showcases such as Bitter End for $10 a night.

One of her first film roles was Holly in the classic *Badlands* (1973); she followed this with an iconic, Oscar-nominated performance as *Carrie*, (1976), the humiliated prom queen who goes postal with her telekinesis. 1980's *Coal Miner's Daughter* won Spacek the Oscar for her performance as country-music legend Loretta Lynn. She continues to work in film and television.

Spacek and her husband live on a large horse ranch in the foothills of Virginia's Blue Ridge Mountains. They have two grown daughters.

M05

M06

M11

M12

M16

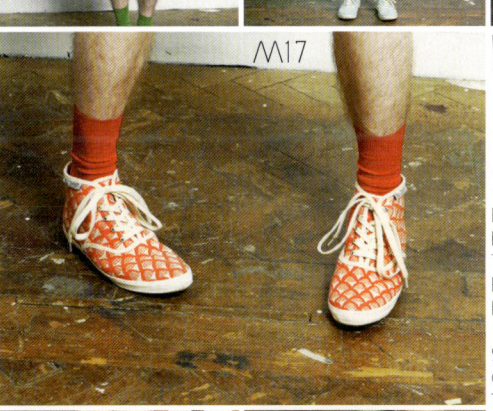

M17

M18

M19

M20

Peter Jensen
«Sissy»
Spring Summer
2006

Press enquiries:
Katie Curran at Cube,
T: +44 20 724-2 54-83
F: +44 20 724-2 54-54
Katie@cubecompany.com

Sales enquiries:
Gerard Wilson,
T: 020 724-9 6894
F: 020 724-9 5858
mail@peterjensenltd.com

Japanese sales:
Zeniya inc.,
T: +81 3 5778 0014
F: +81 3 5778 0015
zeniya@mba.sphere.ne.jp

Photography by Paul Bliss
Model Alex Foxton
Styling by Mattias Karlsson
at intrepid
Men´s shoes by buddahood
Graphic design by Åbäke
Sponsored by TOPSHOP

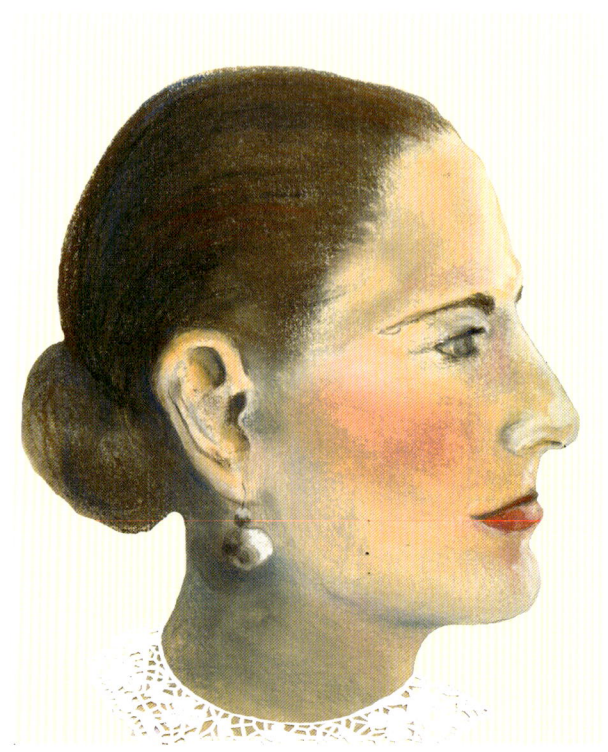

Suzie Foster

HELENA

Helena Rubinstein (December 25, 1870, Krakow, Poland—April 1, 1965, New York City).

Rubinstein's family fostered both her intellectual development and sense of style and elegance; she rewarded them by leaving medical school after two years and rejecting the marriage her parents had arranged. She moved to Australia, and began to distribute a beauty crème that her mother had used, created by Hungarian chemist Jacob Lykusky.

After two years working as a governess, she founded a beauty salon and started to manufacture other cosmetics. Her sisters, Ceska and Manka, joined the business. Rubinstein lived in London and Paris before moving to America. She sold her business to Lehman Brothers in 1928 for $7.3 million, buying it back a year later for about one-fifth of her sale price; it was the Great Depression, but her business thrived. Rubinstein became famous for her art and jewellery collections, among them jewels owned by Catherine the Great.

Rubinstein was about 4 ft 10 inches tall. She died one of the richest women in the world.

Tim, Phil, & I 1989 ©Tina Barney, courtesy Janet Borden, Inc.

TINA

Tina Barney (born 1945, New York City) is an American photographer best known for large-scale portraits of her family and close friends, many of whom are well-to-do denizens of New York and New England.

«Looking at the photographic tableaux of Tina Barney at the Museum of Modern Art, there is a temptation to say. «This is upper-middle-class American life.» The roomy houses are surburban or rural. The people are for the most part healthy, sensitive and decent, and they have grown up with the feeling that outdoor barbecues, big-screen televisions and pink bathrooms are as much God-given rights as air is.» Michael Brenson in the *New York Times*, 26 Jan 1990

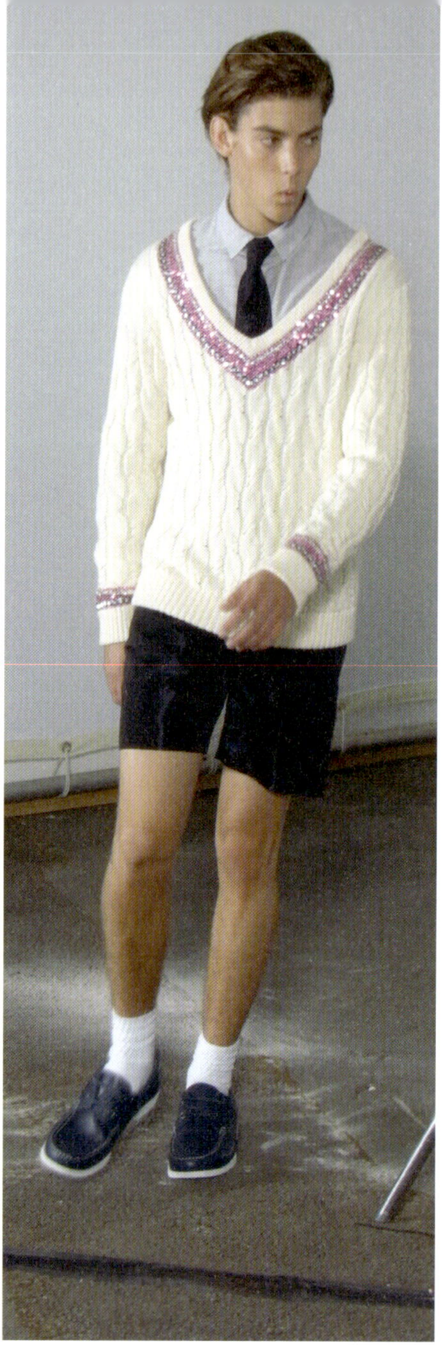

OCTOBER 2007

Amy spends night in cells in Norway for having drugs

AMAR SINGH

[Y] WINEHOUSE and her hus[band] spent the night in police [cells] after being arrested for drug [poss]ession in Norway.
[Wi]nehouse and Blake Fielder-[Civil] were released this morning [and] fined about £350 each for [havi]ng marijuana.
[Pol]ice swooped on the couple at [abou]t 7pm last night at the Radis[son] SAS Hotel Norge Bergen.
[Bo]th were quizzed in the early [hour]s and locked up in separate [cells] at a police station. They were [relea]sed at 7am today. A third [man] was also arrested.
[Ber]gen police confirmed today [that] they confiscated a quantity of [mari]juana found in the singer's [room]. A spokeswoman said: "She [is no] longer at the station. We [relea]sed her after questioning."
[Po]lice confirmed that the [unna]med 25 year-old man was [also] fined after being in the room [and] paid a smaller fine today.

Lars Morten Lothe, a Norwegian prosecutor, confirmed all three were released.
"They were found with seven grams of marijuana," said Mr Lothe. "She's paid the fine, so this thing is over for us now."
Hotel staff alerted police after smelling marijuana smoke emanating from the singer's room yesterday as she enjoyed a day off from her European tour.
A witness said: "There were four police cars parked around the back of the hotel yesterday. They were in and out of her room very swiftly and didn't make a fuss.
"It had been quite obvious that they had been smoking some strong marijuana in their room and guests had complained so the hotel took action."
Winehouse, 24, had been due to perform at the Peer Gynt concert venue in Bergen tonight but the show is set to be cancelled because of her arrest. Police confirmed it was not connected to any incidence of violence and no harder drugs were found in the room.
The arrests come after Winehouse made her touring comeback in Berlin only days ago with a shaky start, when she tripped and staggered as she walked onstage. She also seemed twitchy and nervous, forgetting the first few lines of her cover version of Valerie by the Zutons.
Following her performance at the Mercury Music Awards and Mobo ceremonies in London last month, it was the singer's first full gig since she suffered a drug collapse in August.
Winehouse and Fielder-Civil, who married in May last year, were photographed bloodied and bruised after a bust-up this summer.

"An animated classic..."
★★★★
THE TIMES

Rachel Doyle

CHRISTINA

Christina Oldenburg of Denmark (November 1521, Nyborg–10 December 1590, Tortona, Itlay), younger daughter of Christian II of Denmark and Isabella of Austria, sister of Charles V. In 1533 she was married by proxy to the Duke of Milan. He died two years later.

In 1538, King Henry VIII commissioned portraits of all the noble women of Europe in the hope of finding a bride. Holbein visited Brussels, and for three hours Christina sat for a portrait. She wore mourning dress.

Christina, who was only sixteen, made it clear that she was against the idea—the King´s treatment of his wives was well-known. «If I had two heads,» Christina is supposed to have said, «One should be at the disposal of the King of England.»

In 1541 she married François, Duc de Bar, who succeeded his father as Duc de Lorraine in 1544 and died the year after, leaving Christina Regent of Lorraine. She died in 1590.

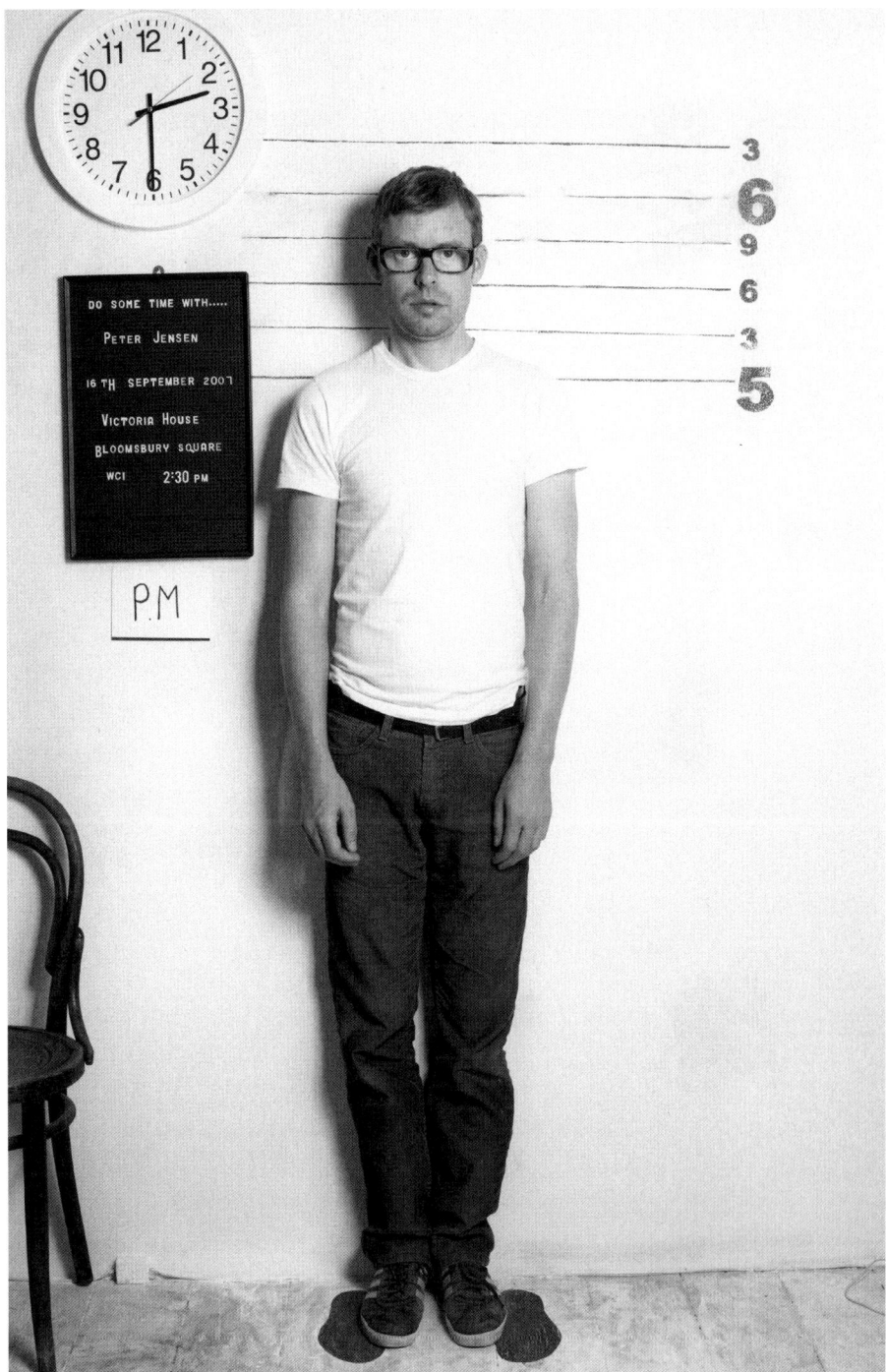

Mink as Taffy Davenport, courtesy Mink Stole

MINK

Nancy Paine Stoll (born August 25, 1947, Baltimore, Maryland), better known by the stage name Mink Stole, is an American actress. She began her career working for director John Waters, and has appeared in all of his feature films to date. She is one of the Dreamlanders, Waters's ensemble of regular cast and crew members.

It is possible to buy autographed photos from her website. She says the following: «Thank you for your order. Your item will be shipped within 3 working days of receipt of confirmation from Paypal. If you have any problems or questions, please email me at minkpix@gmail.com.

PLEASE NOTE: If you wish a personalized autograph, at the time of ordering PLEASE USE THE «SPECIAL INSTRUCTIONS TO MERCHANT» BOX to write YOUR REQUESTED PERSONALIZATION. Otherwise, all photos will be autographed with only my name. Also note that the captions under the photographs as shown in the Gift Shop do not actually appear on the photographs shipped. Again, thank you for your order. Mink Stole»

Julian Drew

CANDICE-MARIE

Candice-Marie (portrayed by Alison Steadman in Mike Leigh's *Nuts in May*, 1976)

Candice-Marie is half of a nature-loving and rather self-righteous couple battling to enjoy what they perceive to be the idyllic camping holiday. Misunderstandings, awkward clashes of values and explosive conflicts occur when less high-minded guests pitch their tents nearby. The usual routine with boyfriend Keith includes performing their own guitar-banjo compositions, preparing healthy vegetarian dinners, and following the Country Code. Candice-Marie—who works in a toy shop—has the personality of an innocent child, one who needs looking after and who is constantly confused and intrigued by her surroundings. She composes little poems and songs, and goes to bed with a fluffy blue hot water bottle called Prudence.

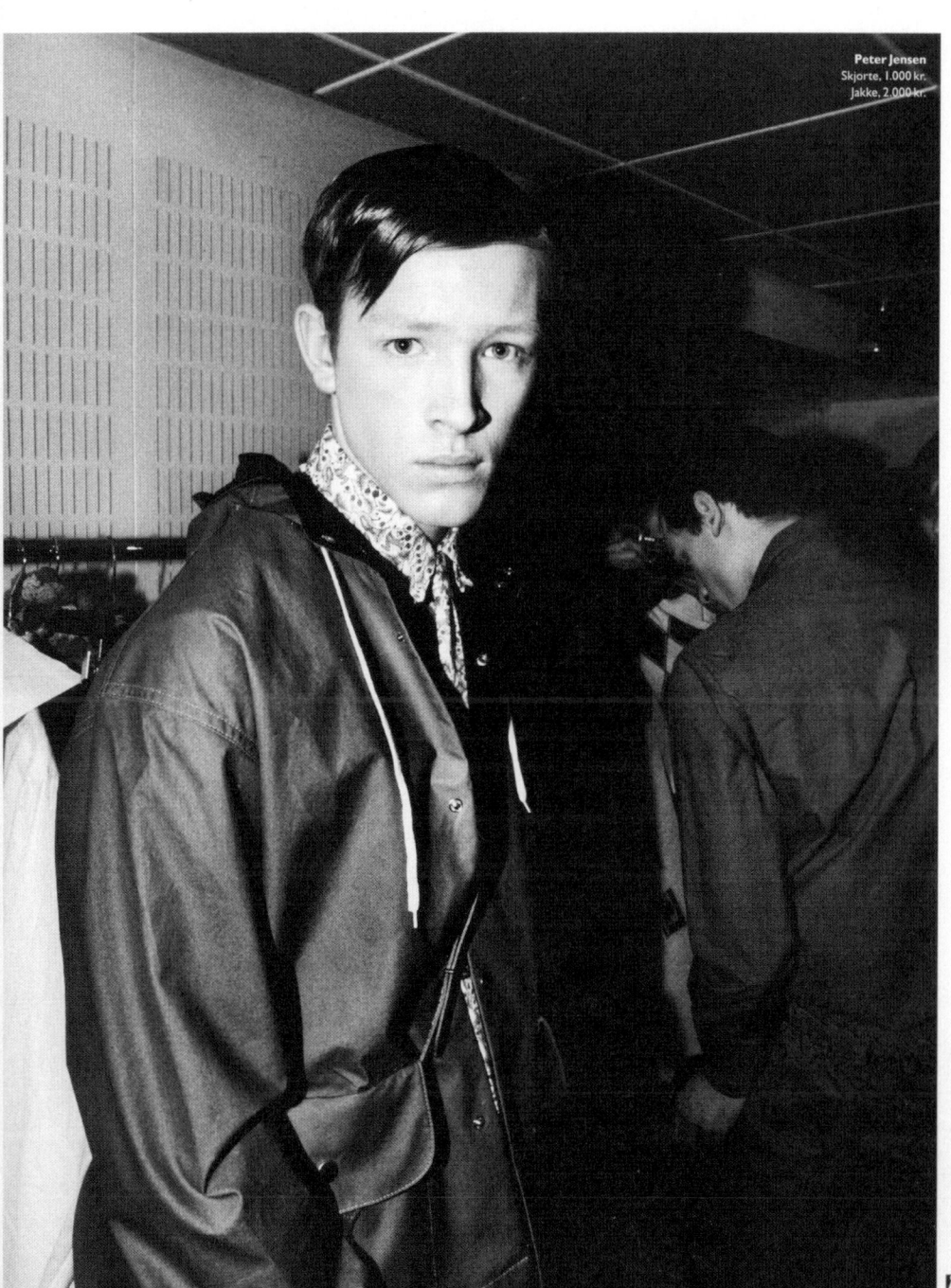

Peter Jensen
Skjorte, 1.000 kr.
Jakke, 2.000 kr.

David Sutton

JODIE

Alicia Christian «Jodie» Foster (born November 19, 1962, Los Angeles, California) is one of the rare examples of a successful child actor whose career didn't dissolve after puberty; after magnificent performances in *Taxi Driver* (1976) and as the infamous Tallulah in *Bugsy Malone* (also 1976), she went on to receive the Academy Award for playing a rape survivor in 1989's *The Accused*.

Perhaps her most famous role came in 1991, as gifted FBI rookie Clarice Starling, assisting in the hunt for a serial killer in *The Silence of the Lambs*.

She was scheduled to graduate in 1984 from Yale University, but the shooting of then-president Ronald Reagan by John Hinckley, Jr. (in which Hinckley's fascination with Foster created adverse publicity for her) caused her to take a semester's leave of absence.

Now also established as a producer and director, Foster is developing a biopic of Leni Riefenstahl. She is the mother of two children, but has never revealed the identity of the children's father(s).

'WHY THESE FIVE WOMEN CHANGED MY LIFE...'

When retail guru Mary Portas agreed to shake up the charity sector for her latest TV series, she had no idea it would change her buying habits forever – and inspire her to start a shopping revolution. Time to get 'shopping neutral' everybody…

"Good evening, Clarice."

"Hello, Doctor Lecter. I hope I'm not intruding. I have some…documents for you to look at."

"You're one of Peter Jensen's, aren't you?"

"I'm just here to show you the looks, Doctor. We'd like your opinion."

"I see. Tell me about this collection, Clarice."

"It's about Jodie. Jodie Foster."

"Another actress? He thinks he can dissect me with this blunt little tool?"

"It's different this time. It's androgynous. It begins with tailoring, damask mini skirt suits with oversized shirts, high waist trousers…."

"You don't have to tell me, Clarice. I see floral jacquards, sequin spot tops, lace-up pencil skirts….this is the Foster of The Accused, of The Hotel New Hampshire, isn't it?"

"We think so. But where is it going, Doctor? Tell me."

"You don't need me to tell you, Clarice. Look inside Your Self."

"What do you mean, Doctor?"

"This collection looks like you too, Clarice. The sporty good looks, the waspy attitude, the tomboy charm. Your grey marl tracksuit with gold foil spot, tailored jackets with shoulder pads. This is a collection for a woman who was never afraid to challenge herself on screen, from the bouncy young girl in Freaky Friday, to the street-wise street-walker of Taxi Driver, the feisty teen in Foxes, right up to the precocious FBI trainee of Silence of the Lambs."

"Quid pro quo, Doctor. Tell me what you see. Tell me about the prints. Or maybe you're afraid to."

"You know what it looks like to me, Clarice? It looks like you've been collaborating with Julie Verhoeven."

"You see a lot, Doctor. It's in the T-shirts, T-shirt dresses, scarves…. They've got her handwriting all over them."

"They're beautiful Clarice. Sometimes you wear leopard-print…but not today."

"It's in the collection, Doctor."

"You dreamed of getting out, didn't you? Getting out, getting all the way to the Oscars party. But you've got nothing to wear."

"You're wrong, Doctor. There are chiffon balloon-sleeve dresses, printed georgette suits. Satin dressing-gown dresses….he might be famous for relaxed and wearable clothing with quirky detailing, but Mr Jensen is getting quite a reputation for party dresses. There's a whole section of evening looks, inspired by Jodie in The Hotel New Hampshire Doctor."

"Mr Jensen knows nothing, Clarice. You know what he looks like to me, with his good bags and his amazing shoes? He looks like a London Fashion Week staple. And the world is certainly more interesting with him in it."

Peter Jensen
«Jytte»

Autumn Winter 2009–2010
Saturday 21 February 2009 at 19:15
P3 University of Westminster
Luxborough Street
London NW1 5LS

Press enquiries:
Starworks
443 Oxford Street
London W1C 2PV
tel. +44 20 7318 04 00
fax. +44 20 7318 04 01
george@starworkslondon.com

Sales enquiries:
Gerard Wilson
T. +44 (0)20 724-9 6894
F. +44 (0)20 724-9 5858
mail@peterjensen.co.uk
gerard@peterjensen.co.uk

Sales Japan:
Zeniya, inc.
Maison Rei 1F, 3-2-8 Higashi
Shibuya-ku, Tokyo
150-0011 Japan
T. +81 3 5778 0014
F. +81 3 5778 0015
zeniya@sky.plala.or.jp

Supported by TOPSHOP

Jytte's family album

JYTTE
«She was born in 1946. She is my dad's little sister, she is number 6 out of 7. She has been married to the same man, Ole, her whole life. She has two boys called Kim and Kurt.

She started smoking when she was around 12, went out dancing from the age of 12. She moved to greenland in her early 20s, lived there for 25 years running the local chip shop and the local taxi company.

She returned to Denmark to Nibe. She then got a job at the local cheese factory and is now retired.»
Peter J.

Proportion

194

«Jytte»

October 21st, 2009

Dear Diary,
I can´t believe it´s 10 years already since we left everything in Denmark. I still remember the day we arrived in Greenland, stepping off the plane, the wind biting my legs; how could I have worn a miniskirt? I don´t know what I did before I got my thigh-high kamik boots!

I must admit it gets lonely out here in Greenland sometimes, the long nights and the freezing winters. Thank goodness I learnt to make those bead capes, it really keeps me busy of an evening.

Today I left my chip-shop, the Drop Inn early. I put on my floral puffa, because I like to look nice despite the weather, and I wandered down to the ocean. The little painted houses look so nice in the snow, it´s magical. I went to Helle´s shop, I got such a lovely velvet dress, printed houndstooth, it shimmers like the seals do lying out on the rocks. I think I´m going to wear it with my checked taffeta coat—which strangely reminds me of the table-cloth in the chip-shop.

When I got home, the kids had made me the most beautiful jewellery—some from pieces of their old school rulers, others in news-paper-maché in the shape of eaten apples, broken hearts and fish bones, they´re ever so creative.

After we had put the little sweet-hearts to bed Ole took me out for dinner. I was wearing my black panné dress, the one with the chiffon frill. We had a glass of schnaps around the fire, wrapped in blankets, it was very cosy.

When we got back to the house, I noticed a postcard; it came from London.

Dear Auntie Jytte, Thank you for the stripey Faroese hat which I wear all the time. Can you please send another one with zig-zags on? Can I come to visit you and uncle Ole? I´m thinking of researching the local fashions for my next collection. I hope everything is fine at the Drop Inn and the taxi company. Lots of love, Peter.

He´s a sweet boy, my nephew, though he´s always had funny tastes, if you ask me. I do hope he gets round to visiting us out here in Nuuk.

Laurie

Spring Summer 2010

By Laurie Simmons and Peter Jensen

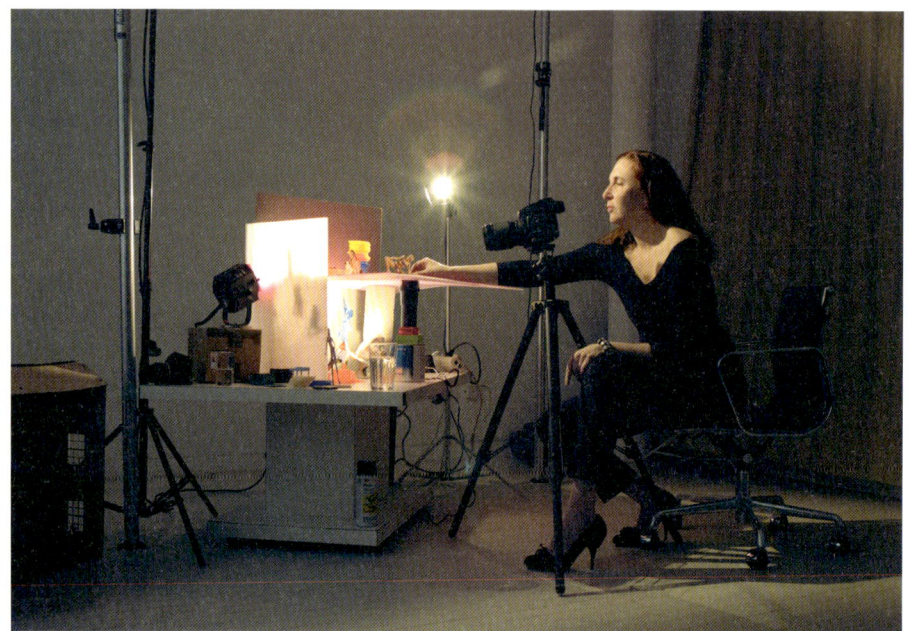

LAURIE

Laurie Simmons (born 1949, Long Island, New York) is an American artist. Simmons's first miniature works, shot in 1976, were black and white images taken in a dollhouse; un-peopled variations of each room in the house, particularly the bathroom. In 1987 Simmons visited the Vent Haven Ventriloquist Museum in Kentucky and over a period of a few years photographed various dummies and props there. More recently she has worked with hyper-realist Japanese sex dolls.

Peter Markus

MURIEL

Dame Muriel Spark, (1 February 1918, Edinburgh – 13 April 2006, Florence) was an award-winning Scottish novelist. She took a course in «commercial correspondence and précis writing», and taught English, an experience that probably informed her most celebrated novel, *The Prime of Miss Jean Brodie* (1961). She also worked as a secretary in a department store.

Her first novel, *The Comforters*, was published in 1957. It featured several references to Catholicism and conversion to Catholicism, although its plot revolved around a young woman who becomes aware that she is a character in a novel.

Spark and her son Robin had a strained relationship. They had a falling out when Robin's Judaism prompted him to petition for his late grandmother to be recognized as Jewish. Spark, a devout Catholic, reacted by accusing him of seeking publicity to further his career as an artist. During one of her last book signings in Edinburgh she responded to an enquiry from a journalist, asking if she would see her son, by saying «I think I know how best to avoid him by now».

Clive Dale

SHELLEY

Shelley Alexis Duvall (born July 7, 1949, Houston, Texas) was working at the cosmetics counter of a department store when Robert Altman cast her in *Brewster McCloud*. Their collaboration continued throughout the 70s, in films such as *Nashville* and *Three Women*, for which she received the Best Actress award at the Cannes Film Festival.

Her next role was opposite Jack Nicholson in Stanley Kubrick's *The Shining* (1980). Nicholson states that Kubrick was «a different director» with Duvall. Notoriously, Kubrick insisted that she and Nicholson perform 127 takes of the distressing baseball bat scene.

In a November 5, 2010 interview with *Mondo Film & Video Guide*, Duvall says: «I wouldn't say I became a recluse. If you Google the meaning, it sounds much worse. I just took time out. I've been acting for over 35 years, it does take a lot out of you. I just needed some me time, and I've loved it. People seem to think I've turned into a recluse who never leaves the house and doesn't communicate with the outside world, that's just not true... I have a quiet life now, I have a lot of animals on my property and look after them; not a crazy cat lady yet though. I write a lot of poetry, would love to publish a book of my work one day. Still get a lot of scripts sent to me, a return to acting is never out of the question.»

Peter Jensen
« Shelley »
SS 2011

Styling: Beth Fenton at Tim Howard
Hair: Neil Moodie at Tim Howard
Make-up: Sally Branka at Julian Watson Agency
Graphic Design: Åbake

UK PRESS
Village Press
The Smokehouse
Smokehouse Yard
4-4 – 4-6 St. John Street
EC1M 4DF London
E: suzi@village-press.com
    press@peterjensen.co.uk
T: +44 (0)20 74 90 7394

DANISH PRESS
Gregersen Communication
Hovedvagtsgade 8
5th floor
1103 Copenhagen K
Denmark
E: andrea@gregersen.cc
T: +45 (0)33 120930

JAPANESE PR/SALES
Diptrics
7-10-10-5F
Minami Aoyama
Minato-ku
Tokyo
Japan 107-0062
T: +81 3 34-09 0089
F: +81 3 34-09 0090
E: mari@diptrics.com

231

PETER JENSEN

Anna Karina

Autumn Winter 2011 presentation

**Tuesday 8 February 2011
10 am – 1 pm
York & Albany
127 – 129 Parkway
London NW1 7PS**

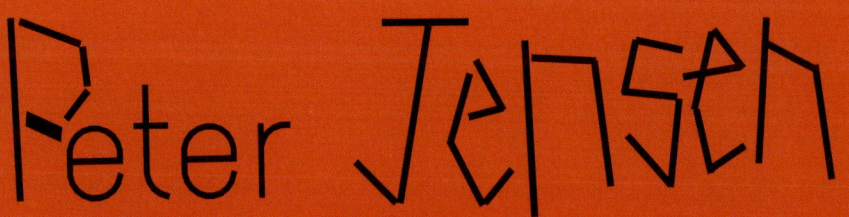

Still from Palmolive advert

ANNA KARINA
Born Hanne Karin Blarke Bayer (1940, Solbjerg, Denmark), it was Coco Chanel who came up with Anna Karina's screen name. A director and screenwriter as well as an actress, Karina is best known as the 60s muse of French New Wave director Jean-Luc Godard.

Karina was 17 when she arrived in Paris—indigent and unable to speak French. Living on the street, she got her break while sitting at the café *Les Deux Magots*: a woman from an advertising agency approached her and asked her to do some photos. She became a successful fashion model, working with Pierre Cardin and Chanel.

Godard first saw Karina in a series of Palmolive ads in which she was in a bathtub covered in soapsuds. He was casting his debut feature film, *A Bout de Souffle* (1960), at the time, and offered her a small part in the film.

She refused when he mentioned that there would be a nude scene, saying «Are you mad?! I was wearing a bathing suit in those ads — the soapsuds went up to my neck. It was in your mind that I was undressed.»

The Life and Times of Peter Jensen
by Susannah Frankel

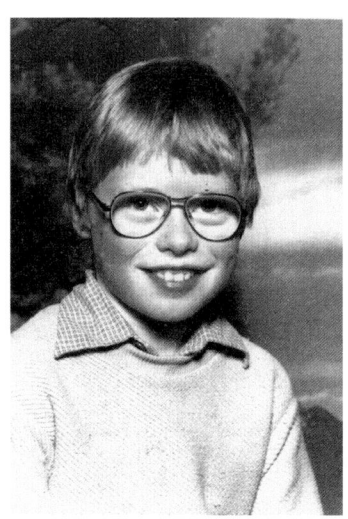

Peter Jensen is sitting in his East London studio at a neatly prepared table where coffee, tea, Jaffa Cakes and a plate of individually packaged biscuits that come all the way from Korea are all positioned perfectly. The latter are a gift from an intern and Jensen says merrily that «they might be disgusting». He seems almost disappointed when I tell him that, actually, they're not. The designer brandishes a stuffed loo roll holder shaped like a cow that hails from the same part of the world. «He gave us this too,» he says, not without pride. We have known each other for a long time now.

Indeed—and he shows me this too—I am honoured to have a place of my own on the collaged walls of his «toilet of fame», a space where guests can ponder at leisure over press cuttings, notes, emails, postcards and such like sent to the designer over the years. Perhaps strangely, we have never really talked about Jensen's life story, and, only rarely, discuss his work. He loves his job, though, he says, but is also obsessed with TV, dogs, cleaning («I don't understand mess at all—it puzzles me») and the sort of gratuitously fatuous gossip that fills the pages of tabloid magazines. *Se og Hor* is his favourite one of these—it's not unlike Denmark's answer to *Now*, apparently, and he buys it immediately he gets off the plane. Recently, the title published an image of *The Killing*'s Detective Lund (aka Sofie Grabol) «in our T-shirt!» It makes a girlish change from her usual, and by now folkloric, Nordic knitwear. The garment in question is small, black and couldn't be more simple were it not for a large pie-crust frill travelling not around the neckline (that would be too straightforward) but horizontally right across the front of it. «It's quite peculiar really. You wouldn't catch DCI Tennison wearing it.» And that's true. As it turns out, Jensen's biography is bizarre to the point of improbable, such are the many twists (to use the word advisedly) and turns that go into its relating.

It all begins, innocently enough, in the tiny fishing village of Logstor, North Jutland, in 1969, although even that is more complicated than it may at first seem.

«I lied about my age for years but now I've gone back to the real one,» Jensen begins. «I'd add a year on, take a year off. I thought it might be fun to create confusion. There are only five thousand people in total living in Logstor. When I grew up my parents had a company that sold kitchens. My dad was a carpenter and my mum was the company secretary—but very much the boss.»

While his parents worked, it was a certain Johanne, who lived across the street, who was responsible for babysitting and, in particular, for taking her young charge to and from school each day. «Johanne was probably in her mid-fifties and basically has no connection to me family wise but, when my dad first moved away from home, he rented a room from her. She didn't have any children of her own, but I grew up with her, and she was really, really good. She couldn't get along with women at all, always had a problem with that. My sister was more with my mum and dad.»

It's safe to say that, this, on the face of it, decidedly odd couple ran joyfully amok, at least partly at the expense of any unsuspecting residents in the vicinity.

«There were no boundaries. She just loved me for everything I did. She had a great sense of humour and absolutely embraced mine. There was an older lady, an 80-year-old woman, Mrs Sogaard, down the road and every time she went for her after-lunch nap we would call her to wake her up. Then, each day after school, we would stage Abba dance competitions. It was me, my friend Michael and my friend Lise Lotte. Lise Lotte was cross-eyed. She had thicker glasses than I do. We had to do a different dance routine each time and then give each other points, vote each other out. It was like X Factor but way before. Johanne made costumes for us. Do you remember those Abba costumes with the animals? We would do them out of sheets and then she would draw animals on them. We wrapped them around us and danced.»

Jensen was very happy, he says, and it was not long after that the seeds of his future profession were more formally sown. «When you're fourteen, in Denmark, you have to do an internship and decide what you want to become. I went to a clothing store. I have no idea why. I remember, though, one day looking out of the window across the street and seeing this man wearing the most fantastic jeans I'd ever seen in my whole life and I just thought: «This is it, I want those jeans so badly.» Following this fashion epiphany, he went home and bleached all his denim in Johanne's bathtub. «Then I started going to evening classes in sewing with all the pensioners. And then we go on to the fat girl who lived next door.»

Ah, the fat girl who lived next door. It is here, with the support of his first patron in effect, that Jensen truly started out on his journey as a designer, cutting out patterns in highly practical jersey and sweat-shirting for his neighbour, who continued to grow larger and larger, and who paid him 20 Danish kroners for an appropriately accommodating top and 15 for an equally generous pair of trousers (around £4 an outfit at the time). «Karina's still around. We're still friends. And she's still fat. She threw all the clothes out, sadly.»

Continuing to struggle elsewhere to fit in with his contemporaries, it wasn't long before Jensen found himself at boarding school, further North still, but the students were, in this case, more cosmopolitan at least. It was, he says, «a special school». Wilson describes it less charitably as «a care home». Whatever, Jensen argues: «I loved it there.»

«Tell her about the girl in the bucket,» Wilson says.

«Oh yes. The girl in the bucket. She was in a wheelchair and very small but with a big head. Because there were no lifts, and she lived on the third floor, they had a bucket and they pulled her up and down in that. The funny thing is that no one really thought it was weird. Lykke was so grumpy. And her name translated from Danish means happiness.»

Jensen stayed at the school in question for a year until, aged 17, he was advised to take a second work placement, this time as a dishwasher in a hotel in the never knowingly glamorous provincial British town of Maidenhead. He travelled to England with his friend, Anita. She went to be a chambermaid there.

«You know, growing up, what I bought was Smash Hits and Number One. I've always been fascinated by English culture and especially the music scene. I very much liked Boy George but I didn't understand any of the humour or the irony of what was said between the lines. I remember trying to translate and thinking: «Nothing he says makes sense. What is this?» Anyway, the hotel was very Mike Leigh [Jensen would soon come to love the work of that film director, naming more than one of his collections after his main protagonists]. The daughter of the man who owned the hotel was like an English rebel, with lipstick and a car, and she would drive us around. I had my own room above the garage and was told all the time by my boss that I was meant to be sharing: «because you're only the dishwasher». I suppose that was the English way of establishing hierarchy. In Denmark you're all equal, which is very boring. Never mind, my claim to fame at the hotel was that I ate Shakin' Stevens' leftovers. A waiter came into the kitchen and said: «Shakin' Stevens is in the hotel and this is his». And so I ate the remains of his chicken. Later, we got the sack actually. We complained so much we were asked to leave.»

Unable to start his degree course until the age of 21—a national stipulation—Jensen next found himself studying again, this time with a group of no less than 89 girls, and focussing on the admittedly none-too-manly pursuit of embroidery.

«There had never been a boy in the school before. I wasn't allowed to live there so I stayed above the bakery. My parents didn't interfere with what I was doing. They never said that I had to be a carpenter like my dad or anything. My dad was very, very laid back. And my mum never understood that any of this would amount to anything. But then neither did I really. I just thought: «this is something I want to do». I'm dyslexic and that's always been a weakness for me. I think I assumed it would be very difficult to go to university and write things because I can't express myself in that way. But sewing was the one thing I knew I could do. On this course, you had to learn how to do all sorts of old-fashioned techniques. I can't say I was particularly good at it, but I understood the method of it. I've always been one of those people who isn't very good at following instructions but who's jealous of people who are. I like things that look proper, but I would get bored halfway through and couldn't fulfil that. After that I moved to Aarhus and went to work at McDonald's. It had to be a drive in so I could smoke out of the window while I was talking into the microphone.»

Jensen went on to learn about traditional tailoring («how to match up checks in a jacket, how to sew in a sleeve by hand, the five hundred ways you can sew in a zip) and graphics (« I was dreadful at life drawing but I can definitely draw well enough that it makes sense, I can use it as a tool), before finally («it was like studying to be a doctor or something») beginning a BA in fashion design at the Denmark Design School in 1994.

«In Scandinavia at that point, and maybe even now, I don't know, fashion was not perceived as serious. The school I went to was known for furniture design, Arne Jacobsen and all those people was all you ever heard about. The head of the college said that the fashion department was full of blonde girls in slip dresses. It was mainly girls although there were two boys in the year above me. I didn't like going to that school. But there was one person, Mrs Veet, who was very old-fashioned. I was terrified of her but I really learned something. She had a belt on, and it was tight—she came from a time when you had a waist—and she wore a turban and diamonds. She was very strict.»

Asked to describe his work during that period, Jensen says, without ceremony: «it was rubbish». But he must have been doing something right because the portfolio he left college with earned him a place on the MA fashion course at Central Saint Martin's, probably the most prestigious of its kind in the world.

«We went on a school trip and visited The Royal College of Art, which seemed too sterile or clean for me, and Saint Martin's. I just remember going into that building and knowing that it was a proper place. Louise (Wilson—MA course director) told me that everything that I'd done was terrible. Obviously. The only thing she liked about me was my glasses and my suitcase. It was like an old 50s suitcase. But I think I got along with her in the interview probably. She was smoking at that time. All the way through. And I remember saying. «can I have a cigarette?» and she said, «no, it's only my favourite students who are allowed to smoke in my office». And I thought: «if I get accepted I'm going to remember that». And I did eventually have a cigarette with her in her office, yes.»

Jensen's was a fine year. Among his classmates were Emma Cook, Roksanda Ilincic, Russell Sage, Adam Entwistle, Siv Stoldal and Estrella Archs. Jensen studied menswear, graduating, in 1999, with distinction and, with at least some of his contemporaries, ushered in a new school of fashion, which was quieter than the power-driven, pointy lapelled and crescent-moon shouldered one that came before it. Not that it was any less subversive, but any irreverence—and in fact that was extreme—lay in an ironic and subtly disruptive viewpoint and one that was at times even openly comedic.

«My time at Saint Martin's was the absolute educational best,» Jensen says. «I remember Louise saying to me in my interview: «one thing I don't understand about you is why you don't design what you wear yourself». I was wearing a pair of vintage black wool trousers and a white T-shirt. And no one had ever said that to me. In Denmark you are removed from what it is you wear yourself in your work. But that made sense to me. What I needed to do became clear.»

Julie Verhoeven, Jane Shepherd and Fabio Piras were among his teachers. The principle influence was deconstruction—Margiela menswear, which clearly informs Jensen's aesthetic, was relatively new. «I think my degree collection was a bit like that, but also Scandinavian. There were a lot of jumpers. They were hand-knitted by my mum. And it was quite commercial, easy to wear. You know, trousers with a nice pocket detail.»

And, of course, although it was entitled «Marianne» (as in Faithfull) it featured a

Mary Bell shirt which became the first in a long line of references to less than conventionally lovely women that would become increasingly integral to his process. «That's probably where something quite dry comes in,» Jensen says for his part, and he is nothing if not master of the understatement. «There was a new book about her that I was reading at the time.»

«Peter and I met because we were both asked to model for Peter Cash, one of the BA menswear students,» says Wilson. «We had to be done up like ventriloquists' dummies and we did it three times because they have the internal show, then the press show and then he was in the gala show. So we spent many hours having our shiny faces slathered in Eight Hour Cream and getting bits of itchy ginger wig hair glued to our eyebrows. It created a bond.»

After graduation, Jensen went straight into business designing his own label in partnership with the Italian producer/distributor, Eo Bocci. «They came to college just before we finished and ten of us were chosen to show our collection. There were two menswear designers—me and

Siv—and obviously we thought we didn't have a hope in hell. With the womenswear designers you could almost see the ambition coming out of their pores. They had models and everything and we were just sitting there like a pair of children. They came back again after the final show and they had chosen me but by then I had sold my whole collection. I had nothing left. It went so quick, you know. Too quick. This was April and by June I had done my first collection for them. I think that what they had hoped for was an instant superstar of some sort and I was completely the wrong person for that. I didn't know anything. I would sit there in production meetings in Italy and I just thought I don't even know what this is. I was with them for three seasons. I did one show in Paris. I had a press office, Totem. But it was all very scattered really.»

«And not at all glamorous,» Wilson adds.

Mary Miles Minter (Autumn/Winter 2001/2) was the name of Peter Jensen's first collection for women, although he always continued to design and show menswear alongside. He says today that he moved in that direction simply to «try something new». The conceit of the muse embraced everything from the fundamentally flawed to the beautifully regal, and from the blue-blooded American to the sort of lower middle class English woman whose essentially banal existence would have proved far from obvious fodder for a British-born designer. Jensen studies these women with all the intensity of an obsessive fan.

«They're mostly a bit damaged aren't they?» Wilson points out.

«Yes, they are,» Jensen continues. «And, yes, I do think that's funny. And that's difficult for me to explain.»

The exception that proves the rule is Christina (of Denmark, Autumn/Winter 2007): «I don't think Christina of Denmark was funny. She was a serious inspiration and she's not damaged, she's strong.

Sometimes any interpretation is literal—in Jodie (Foster, Spring/Summer 2009) a model wears a grey jogging suit just like the one the actor has on in the opening scene of Silence of the Lambs; models in Sissy (Spacek, Spring/Summer 2006) sport shirtwaister dresses and oversized freckles. Other times it's more lateral, capturing a mood— anything from buttoned up Hamptons preppy to English country dowdy and with more than a few «weird, camp monsters» thrown in for good measure. «I don't think it's ever a question of laughing at them,» Jensen says of his relationship with his muses. «It's always laughing with them.»

«I think our design is quite unremarkable,» says Wilson attempting to sum up the Peter Jensen aesthetic in a manner that might, under certain circumstances, not unreasonably be described as self-deprecating, were it not for the fact that he clearly means it. «We like everyday things. We're not drawn to the sequinned ball gown but to the T-shirt. There's an attraction to the everyday but in a slightly odd way.»

«I think,» adds Jensen, «looking back, it's gone very slowly compared to some of our contemporaries in the business. Some of them have been successful overnight, which, at times, has made me very jealous. But that comes down to what we do. It's sometimes to do with our designs. Other people have approached it in a much more fashion-y way. «What are you interested in this season?» «Well, it's all about the fabrics.» I've never understood that. Not that I want to be intellectual. But I've never understood talking like that. «This season I'm doing very sexy.» You know.»

Stating the obvious: Jensen himself has never uttered these particular words.

«I'm more anti-sex than you are though,» says Wilson. «Peter actually likes breasts. I think it's a slightly menswear approach. The way that you draw, which is mostly how the things are designed, is flat. You're not thinking about the body.»

«It never comes right when I design on the body,» Jensen elaborates. «I don't think that's what we're good at. I can see the beauty in it when somebody does it really well. That's a skill and it can be done really brilliantly but, it's true, our clothes are probably quite flat.»

Here's Wilson again: «It's simple without being minimal and quite basic sometimes but it's odd too isn't it? I think often we're trying to do something quite basic but it always ends up odd. So, something we might see as utility is in fact strange. We're just trying to make a shirt that looks like a shirt, that is just unremarkable but it rarely ends up that way.»

If the clothes may, on a certain level, be basic —if always with idiosyncrasies that ensure they stand out in the crowd almost despite themselves—the method of presentation has on occasion been more conceptually oriented. Take Cindy (Sherman, Autumn/Winter 2004). As a starting point, Jensen invited his most important collaborators—stylists, design assistants, friends and so forth—to come into the studio for a day and pick clothes of his design from rails to make a single look. Hair and make-up—think Disney with a suitably perverse injection of Northern European wit—rendered models almost unrecognisable. Then there was Tonya (Harding, Spring/Summer 2005) that saw a troupe of real ice-skaters, aged no more than around 14 and pink-faced from the exertion, belting around a less than salubrious rink in West London in frilly knickers stamped with everything from tiny apples and pears to potatoes and turnips.

«I think we use the muses as a working tool more than anything, don't we?» Jensen argues. «It starts a research process. It doesn't have to define a collection; it's a reference point, giving us something to go back to. Sometimes our choice of muse is related to what we're thinking about designing, and sometimes it totally isn't. Sometimes it's easy because I've read about them and I like them but more often it's difficult—it's such a long and winding story.»

And, in that, it mirrors both the life and work of the designer in question quite neatly. For all his less-than-establishment stance, after ten years and with both main line and resort women's and men's collections, Peter Jensen has a successful business and one run, mostly—and unusually—independently and on his own terms. «I'm dreadful at networking I'm one of the most awkward people,» he says.

At least partly for that reason and whichever way one chooses to look at it, Jensen's has been far from what is known in fashion circles as «a meteoric rise to fame».

«It's been meandering,» the designer confirms. «Other people have a business plan. They think: «I'm going to make these clothes, for this market». It never really occurred to us to do it like that.»

MUSIC INDEX

2001_AW_Mary Miles Minter
    String quartet

2002_SS_Mildred
    Shit & Chanel

2002_AW_Emma
    show music by Emma Cook
    The Cramps — *Human Fly*
    Talking Heads (Distortion Mix)
    — *Take Me To The River*
    Absolute Body Control (Brian Eno)
    — *Baby's On Fire*
    ESG — *Moody*
    Le Tigre — *Hot Topic*
    The Amboy Dukes — *Baby Please Don't Go*
    Link Wray — *Rumble*
    The Flamin' Groovies — *Shake Some Action*

2003_SS_Olga
    show music by Fabio Almeida
    Survivor — *Eye of the Tiger*
    Black Lodge— *Blood/Brass*
    Elk City — *Freeze Over Eight*
    Toy Flotation Warning — *Losing Carolina*
    Ravel— *Bolero*
    Cherrystones —
    Max Tundra — *Cake*
    + samples of applause and gymnastic score marks

2003_AW_Nancy
    show music by Fabio Almeida
    Merricks — *Burn Munich Down*
    Scott Walker — *The Girls and the Dogs*
    3rd Man soundtrack by Anton Karas
    — *Harry Lime Theme*
    Frank Ifield — *I Remember You*
    Real Tuesday Weld — *Bath Time in Clerkenwell*
    Cheesy instrumental version of Elvis
    — *C'mon Sugar*
    + samples of various animal noises

2004_SS_Gertrude
    show music by Fabio Almeida
    Hasey Fantesy — *John Wayne is Big Leggy*
    Boney M — *Night Flight to Venus*
    Bow Wow Wow — *Wild in the Country*

2004_AW_Cindy
    show music by Ann-Sofie Back
    Dad rock (Ann-Sofie's description)

2005_SS_Tonya
    show music by Fabio Almeida
    The Royal Orchestra plays:
    (Beatles) — *Get Back*
    (Tchaikovsky)—*Waltz* from *Sleeping Beauty*
    (Four Tops) — *Reach Out, I'll be There*
    (Survivor)— *Eye of the Tiger*
    (Rossini)— *Wlliam Tell Overture*
    (Wagner) — *Ride of the Vakyries*
    (Gounod)—*Faust*
    (Prokofiev) —*Peter and the Wolf*
    + samples of crowd cheering etc

2005_AW_Fanny
    show music by Fabio Almeida
    Walt Disney music — *Dumbo*
    Klaxons — *Clap Clap Song*
    Andy Votel — *Gentle Man Thief*
    Soundtrack from *La Dolce Vita*
    Broadcast— *Lunch Hour Pops*
    M83 — *Lower Your Eyelids to Die with the Sun*

2006_SS_Sissy
    show music by Jerry Bouthier
    Theme music from Terence Malik
    movie *Badlands* :
    Carl Orff— *Gassenhauer*
    KLF — *Chill Out* album
    June Carter Cash (as a child)
    Pino Donaggio — *Carrie*
    Whomadewho — *Space for Rent*

2006_AW_Helena
    show music by Jerry Bouthier
    Plaid — *Scoobs*
    Fred Astaire — *Puttin on the Ritz*
    Marilyn Monroe — *Diamonds are a Girl's Best Friend*

2007_SS_Tina
    show music by Jerry Bouthier
    Steel drums band — *Killing Me Softly*
    The Cure — *Boys Don't Cry*
    Dusty Springfield — *Always Something There To Remind Me*
    Extracts from an interview with Tina Barney

2007_AW_Christine
    show music by Jerry Bouthier
    Michel Legrand and the soundtrack to
    Jacques Demy's — *Peau D'Ane*
    Christine Aguilera — *Beautiful*

2008_SS_Mink
    show music by Jerry Bouthier
    Mink Stole — *I wish I had a gun*
    Smashing Pumpkins (The Carpenters)
    — *Superstar*

2008_AW_Candice-Marie
    show music by Jerry Bouthier
    Intro: Mike Leigh — *Nuts In May*
    The Grimethorpe Colliery Band —
    The Rhythmic Danube
    Holger Czukay — *The Photo Song*
    The Peppers — *Pepper Box*
    Acid Brass — *Pacific 202*
    Michel Legrand — *Les Jumeaux*
    Fred Viola — *Hogwash*
    Acid Brass — *Let's Get Brutal*
    The Sounds Of Tomorrow — *Space Child*
    Finale: The Band Of Yorkshire Imperial
    Metals — *Hello Goodbye*

2009_SS_Jodie
    show music by Jerry Bouthier / JBAG
    David Bowie — *Shake It*
    Janis Ian — *Fly Too High*
    Hollywood Mon Amour — *Cat People*
    Janis Ian — *At Seventeen*
    Detektiv Byran — *Nattopett*
    Hollywood Mon Amour —
    Together In Electric Dreams
    Finale: Darlington — *Jodie Foster*

2009_AW_Jytte
    show music by Jerry Bouthier / JBAG
    Mary Schneider — *Yodelling Overtures*
    Vampire Weekend — *M79*
    Anne Linnet — *Humorsang*
    I Monster — *The Blue Wrath*
    Sia — *Buttons (CSS remix)*
    Dan Deacon — *Surprise Stefani*
    Finale: Anne Linnet— *Sigurd*

2010_SS_Laurie
    show music by Jerry Bouthier
    Produced by Jerry Bouthier
    & Andrea Gorgerino / JBAG
    Ken Thorne & His Orchestra —
    Sur La Route Qui Va
    Michel Legrand & His Orchestra
    — *The Last Time I Saw Paris*
    John Morris — *The Elephant Man*
    Michel Legrand & His Orchestra —
    La Vie En Rose
    Michel Legrand & His Orchestra
    — *April In Paris*
    Nelson Riddle & His Orchestra
    — *Que Reste-t-il De Nos Amours*
    David Rose — *Like Young*
    The City Of Prague Philharmonic Orchestra
    & James Fitzpatrick
    — *Edward Scissorhands main title*
    — *Ice Dance*
    Michel Legrand & His Orchestra — *La Seine*

2010_AW_Muriel
    live music by Nina Persson & Nathan Larson
    Kristy Mccoll — *They Don't Know About Us*
    John Lennon — *Love*
    Todd Rundgren — *I Saw The Light*
    Patsy Cline — *I Fall To Pieces*
    Wreckless Eric — *Whole Wide World*
    Neil Young — *I Am A Child*
    Big Star —*You And Your Sister*
    Lou Reed — *Satellite Of Love*

2011_SS_Shelley
    show music by Jerry Bouthier / JBAG
    Patrick Juvet — *I Love America*
    Passengers — *Hot Leather*
    Bebu Silvetti — *Spring Rain*
    Teebs — *While You Dooo*
    Bud Powell & Ray Noble & His Orchestra —
    Midnight the Stars and You
    Voyage — *Souvenirs*
    Instant Funk — *I Got My Mind Made Up*
    Au Revoir Simone — *Another Likely Story
    (Aeroplane remix)*
    Firefly — *Love (Is Gonna Be On Your Side)*
    D. D. Sound — *Burning Love*
    Kano — *Now Baby Now*

2011_AW_Anna-Karina
    playlist remembered by Shirley Kurata
    Anna Karina — *Sous le Soleil Exactement*
    The Go-Betweens — *The Sound of Rain*
    Les Paul — *It's only a Paper Moon*
    The Fleetwoods — *Mr. Blue*

着だおれ方丈記

第71回　ピーター・イェンセン

写真・文＝都築響一

タバコは吸うけどベランダで、食事は３食とも外食で、部屋ではお湯もめったに沸かさない、とにかく真っ白でミニマルなスタイルが好きという24歳の彼。武蔵小杉駅から徒歩10分のアパートには、ターンテーブルと、テクノ・ミュージックのレコードと、ピーター・イェンセンの服しかない感じだ。ピーター・イェンセンを集め出したのは２年半ほど前。それまではマルジェラが好きだったりしたものの、特定のブランドに入れ込むこともなかったが、代官山のセレクトショップで、ピーター・イェンセンの印象的なプリントに出会う。一目で気に入り、のめりこんでいくうちに、雑誌の巻末に掲載されていた問い合わせ先に電話してみたら、繋がったのは卸会社。ショップじゃないけど、少しでも多くの洋服を見られるのではないかと、住所を聞き出し乗り込んだ、かなりの行動派だ。結局、会社の代表から熱意を買われて、ついには転職。いまでは社販でピーター・イェンセンの商品を購入できるようになったため、デザイナーと同じく細身の彼のコレクションは、まだまだ増えそうな様子。ちなみに洋服とレコードを買うために切り詰めるのは、もっぱら食費だそう。食にはあまり執着がなくて、「３食牛丼でも平気」。でも朝はかならず喫茶店でコーヒーを飲むことに決めているとか。

He smokes, but only out on the veranda. Takes three meals a day, but always eats out. Hardly ever boils water in his apartment. Whatever, this 24-year-old takes his pure white minimal style seriously. Living halfway to Yokohama, a short 10-minute walk from Musashi Kosugi Station, his sole possessions seem to be his turntables, techno music records and Peter Jensen clothes. He began collecting Jensen two and a half years ago. He liked Martin Margiela before that, though not enough to really zoom in on the brand, when one day at an import shop in Daikanyama he came across an impressive Jensen print and was taken at first sight. Meanwhile, his curiosity piqued, he found a contact number at the back of a magazine and rang up what proved to be a wholeseller. It wasn't a shop, but at least he could see more of the clothes; he asked the address and rode out to have a look. In any case, the company rep bought his enthusiasm, and soon he switched jobs. Now that he can buy Peter Jensen products in-house, his collection keeps growing while he himself stays active as the designer. Just for the record, literally, his money for music and clothes all comes from trimming food expenses. He's not fussy about what he eats: "Beef bowl three times a day is fine." And yet he does insist on his cafe routine each and every morning.

Translation ALFRED BIRNBAUM

```
09:00   起床
        Wake up
        喫茶店でコーヒーを飲む
        Coffee at a cafe
11:00   出社
        Head to the office
23:00   帰宅
        Go home
02:00   就寝
        Sleep
```

HAPPY VICTIMS Vol.71
PETER JENSEN
Photography & Text KYOICHI TSUZUKI

	PHOTOGRAPHY/PRINT	STYLING	PUBLICATION
Endpapers	Kathryn Dale		
p.25	Roksanda Ilincic		
p.27–28	Peter Jensen Studio		
p.29	Peter Mann	Charlotte Mann	Tank, issue 6, vol. 2, November 2001
p.30	John Spinks	Jonathan Kaye	Sleazenation, January/February 2002
p.31–34	Chris Moore	Tom Murphy	
p.37	Chris Moore	Jonathan Kaye	
p.38	Marc Van Lengen	Luke Day	attitude, February 2002
p.39–40	Åbäke		
p.41 top	Chris Moore	Jonathan Kaye	
p.41 bottom	Takay	Mark Antony	i-D, December/January 2001
p.42	Peter Jensen Studio		
p.43	Åbäke		
p.47 top	Åbäke	Lucy Ewing	
p.47 bottom	Peter Mann		
p.48	Åbäke		
p.49	Peter Mann		
p.50–51			The Independent Review, 8 August 2002
p.52	Robert Wyatt	Lucy Ewing	i-D, May 2001
p.55	Sean + Seng with Åbäke		Tank, issue 5, vol. 3, 2005
p.56–57	Peter Mann		
p.58	Jay Brooks		The Guardian, The Guide, 22 May 2004
p.59–60	Chris Moore	Lucy Ewing	
p.61	Dirk Sieden Schwan	Cathy Edwards	Dazed & Confused, March 2003
p.62	Andreas Larsson	Ann-Sofie Back	Dazed & Confused, April 2003
p.65	David Woolley	Lee Holmes	The Independent, 1 January 2004
p.66	Chris Moore	Lucy Ewing	
p.67	Peter Jensen Studio		
p.68	Peter Mann		
p.69	Åbäke		
p.71	Chris Moore	Lucy Ewing	
p.72–73	Åbäke		
p.74–75	Chris Moore	Lucy Ewing	
p.76	Paul Bliss		
p.79	Hisashi	Lucy Ewing	
p.80–81	Peter Jensen Studio		
p.82	Robert Montgomery	Julie Telfer	Dazed & Confused, August 2004
p.83–85	Dennis Schoenberg	Lucy Ewing	
p.86 left	Jody Barton		
p.86 right	Peter Mann		
p.87	Jody Barton		
p.88	Dennis Schoenberg	Lucy Ewing	i-D, September 2004
p.91	Chris Moore	Lucy Ewing	
p.92	Paul Bliss		
p.93–95	Chris Moore	Lucy Ewing	
p.96–97	Paul Bliss		
p.98			Loaded Fashion
p.101	Paul Bliss		i-D, July 2005

	PHOTOGRAPHY/PRINT	STYLING	PUBLICATION
p.102	Kathryn Dale		
p.103			Collezioni, Autumn/Winter 2005
p.104–105	Paul Bliss		
p.106	Daniel Smith		Marie Claire, September 2005
p.107			The Sun, 17 February 2005
p.108–109	Peter Mann		
p.110	Chris Moore	Lucy Ewing	
p.113–114	Mauro Cocilio		The Independent, 24 December 2005
p.115	Chris Moore	Lucy Ewing	
p.116–1117	Paul Bliss	Mattias Karlsson	
p.118–119	Chris Moore	Lucy Ewing	
p.120	Paul Bliss	Lucy Ewing	
p.121			Showstudio
p.122–124	Jane McLeish-Kelsey	Lucy Ewing	Lula, vol. 1, Fall 2005
p.127–128	Peter Mann		
p.130–131	Chris Moore	Lucy Ewing	
p.132–133	Peter Mann		
p.134–135	Robert Wyatt	Lucy Ewing	
p.136			So-en Magazine
p.137	Åbäke		
p.139 top	Tina Barney, courtesy Janet Borden, Inc. **Mark, Amy, & Tara 1983**		
p.139 bottom	Peter Mann	Beth Fenton	
p.140	Chris Moore		
p.142–144	Peter Mann	Beth Fenton	
p.144–145			Evening Standard, 19 October 2007
p.146 top left	Wendy Bevan	Gemma Hayward	The Independent, 6 May 2007
p.146 top right	Dan Jackson	Joanna Schlenzka	Dazed & Confused, April 2007
p.146 bottom	Peter Mann	Beth Fenton	
p.149	Robert Wyatt	Lucy Ewing	10, Winter 2007
p.150	Chris Moore	Beth Fenton	
p.152	Kathryn Dale		
p.153–154	Chris Moore	Beth Fenton	
p.155	Glen Erler	Sophia Neophitou	10, Winter 2007
p.156	Chris Moore	Beth Fenton	
p.157	Paul Bliss	Andy Hillman	
p.159	Pierre Bailly	Cathy Kasterine	i-D, March 2008
p.160	Robert Wyatt	Lucy Ewing	Sunday Time Style, June 2008
p.160 right	Chris Moore	Beth Fenton	
p.161–162	Charlotte Mann		
p.163	Chris Moore	Beth Fenton	
p.164–165	Peter Mann		
p.166	Chris Moore	Beth Fenton	
p.169	Yvan Rodic		www.facehunter.com
p.171	Tim Walker	Kate Phelan	Vogue, December 2008
p.172	Shoji Fujii	Jacob K	
p.173			Arena (DK)
p.174–177	Paul Bliss	Beth Fenton	
p.178	Åbäke		
p.181	Max Farago	Beth Fenton	Art direction: Tom Watt

	PHOTOGRAPHY/PRINT	STYLING	PUBLICATION
p.182 left	Chris Moore	Beth Fenton	
p.182 right	Kate Rodgers & Rod Edmond		Dazed Digital
p.183 top	Peter Mann		
p.183 bottom	Kate Rodgers & Rod Edmond		Dazed Digital
p.184			Grazia, issue 220
p.185 left	Peter Mann		
p.185 right	Chris Moore	Beth Fenton	
p.186	Chris Moore	Beth Fenton	
p.187–188	Max Farago	Beth Fenton	Art direction: Tom Watt
p.191	Tim Walker	Kate Phelan	Vogue, December 2009
p.192	Chris Moore	Beth Fenton	
p.193	Tim Walker		
p.194 top	Roger Rich	Sam Ranger	b store magazine, issue 1
p.194 bottom	Chris Moore	Beth Fenton	
p.195	Jytte		
p.196–197	Kathryn Dale		
p.198–200	Chris Moore	Beth Fenton	
p.201	Laurie Simmons	Beth Fenton	Layout: Tom Watt
p.203–214	Laurie Simmons	Beth Fenton	Layout: Tom Watt
p.215	Nina B		
p.217–219	Dan Lecca	Beth Fenton	
p.220–221	Bernard Elsmere		
p.222	Dan Lecca	Beth Fenton	
p.223–224	Bernard Elsmere		
p.225	Åbäke		
p.227	Kathryn Dale		
p.228	Robert Wyatt	Lucy Ewing	Sunday Style, 24 March 2011
p.229–232	Dan Lecca	Beth Fenton	
p.235–242	Autumn de Wilde	Shirley Kurata	
p.243	Peter Jensen family album		
p.247	Peter Mann		
p.252	American tourist	Peter Jensen & Gerard Wilson in Greenland	
p.266–267	Kyoichi Tsuzuki		Ryoku Tsushin

SET DESIGN

Tina, Muriel, Charlotte Mann
Fanny, Sissy, Helena: Andy Hillman

PRESS RELEASE COPY

Alex Foxton

INVITES, LOOKBOOKS & ILLUSTRATIONS

Åbäke

THANK YOU

To past and present staff, interns, photographers, stylists, models, hair & make-up artists and everybody that has helped Peter Jensen.

For more information please visit: www.peterjensen.co.uk